THIS MIGHT GET ME FIRED

THIS MIGHT GET ME FIRED

A MANUAL FOR THRIVING IN THE CORPORATE ENTREPRENEURIAL UNDERGROUND

GREGORY LARKIN

THIS MIGHT GET ME FIRED
*A Manual for Thriving in the Corporate
Entrepreneurial Underground*

ISBN 978-1-5445-1071-2 *Paperback*
       978-1-5445-1070-5 *Ebook*

To my big brother, Jake, and his twin sister-in-law, Pauline.

CONTENTS

INTRODUCTION 9

1. THE INNOVATION THAT'S NECESSARY IS NEVER AUTHORIZED...17

2. IF YOU CAN'T LAUNCH IN EIGHT WEEKS, YOU NEVER WILL......31

3. THE GODFATHER 57

4. THE SECRET SOCIETY 71

5. GUERRILLA VALIDATION 81

6. INNOVATION ON TOUR SECRETLY 97

7. THE RIGHT EXIT AND ITS EVIL TWIN.................................. 113

8. COURAGE AND RISK 127

ACKNOWLEDGEMENTS... 131

ABOUT THE AUTHOR...133

INTRODUCTION

THE CHASM OF COURAGE

Watching Tom try to get fired was illuminating. The hidden truth of why some corporate innovation succeeds and most fails came into stark relief.

The setting was a slick hotel ballroom in LA where Tom, a product innovation executive at PricewaterhouseCoopers PwC, demoed a virtual financial advisor to about a hundred tech executives. They were amazed. After the presentation, Tom migrated from one huddle of executives to the next, bathing in accolades and planning follow-up meetings.

Kelly, a Microsoft executive, clinked Tom's glass and said, "We feel like you've planted a flag where we all need to go. We're excited." He then patted Tom's shoulder and squeezed it to emphasize the point. The tactile gesture was out of character for Kelly, who seemed like he probably didn't hug his own kids.

Clayton, a senior partner at PwC, was standing next to Kelly and parroted his praise, "We're excited, too." Clayton then said to Tom that there was someone he wanted him to meet. He steered him out of the room, and once they were a few feet away, he narrowed his brow and glared at him. "Are you fucking crazy?! Microsoft is *my* client. Oracle is *my* client," he hissed through clenched teeth. "You don't return my phone calls this morning. And instead of a PowerPoint deck—it's a product launch?!" His face was red, and his eyes were piercing.

This moment of confrontation is often when great products get killed for not following protocol. It's when entrepreneurs inside big organizations—intrapreneurs— finally submit to their reprogramming and become banal and deferential. Or they are purged from the organization.

But something made Tom respond differently. "Clayton, if you think you can do better, then go back inside, tap a spoon on your glass, and announce to all of them that I'm fired. Tell that to all the other partners who need this product to win. In fact, I'm actually begging you to do exactly that. 'Cause this is a waste of my time. I'm sick of this shit."

Tom then stepped aside like a bellhop in a five-star hotel and motioned for Clayton to walk back into the room and make the announcement.

Clayton's face morphed from venomous to scared and placating. He motioned with his hands for Tom to please calm down. "I'm sorry Tom. It's on me to work more closely with you to make this work. I just didn't appreciate that this was being built." He winced as he pronounced the word built. "Let's go back inside and kiss some ass."

Clayton retired two months later.

I was part of the team that built the product with Tom. Afterward, we would go on to launch six more breakout products inside of PwC, one of the oldest, most conservative management consultancies in the world. It was more thrilling and impactful than any startup I ever worked with.

For twelve years, I had worked with every innovation, agile, and design thinking framework I could get my hands on. I practically memorized *The Lean Startup*, *The Innovator's Dilemma*, *Habit-Forming Products*, *The Scrum Manifesto*, and every other innovation bible I could read. I used artificial intelligence, the blockchain, virtual reality, and other cutting-edge technologies. They all promised to "revolutionize" and "transform."

But the only time they actually fulfilled that promise was when someone like Tom stepped forward and said, "Building this might get me fired. And I'm doing it anyway." The most powerful innovation tools in the world were dormant assets when they weren't plugged into the power grid of courage.

TEN YEARS AGO I'D HAVE HAD YOU KILLED

Courage, like the bold stand that Tom took, is one of the most misunderstood, unheralded, and essential acts of entrepreneurship. But not long ago, it could have gotten you killed. More specifically, someone like Clayton could have made a few phone calls and placed you on a "Do Not Hire" blacklist. It made a lot of sense for someone who was born with the wiring of an entrepreneur to keep their mouth shut, try to fit in, and obediently endure the torture of corporate intransigence. Your fears of never making money again, having a bad reference, and professional ignominy all had some basis in reality.

Back then, once a company got big, it stayed big. And once an executive reached a certain level of seniority, they focused on enlarging their fiefdom. In 1979, the average tenure of a company in the S&P 500 was thirty-six years. Today, it is fourteen years and falling fast. Not long ago, it seemed more sensible to work for Barnes & Noble rather than the startup that eventually drove it into bankruptcy,

Amazon. It was more prudent to accept a lucrative offer from Blockbuster than a riskier, equity-laden offer from Netflix. It appeared safer to be a sycophant in the executive team of J.C. Penney than in the roller coaster of a new company called eBay in a new industry called e-commerce.

For a long time, your goal as a responsible grown-up was to find a job and endure it for life.

But times have changed. It is more of a risk now to be placed on the innovation blacklist—where you've become so fluent in the archaic ways of operating in an old company that you're no longer relevant in the modern economy.

THIS BOOK IS MEANT TO AWAKEN THE DORMANT ENTREPRENEUR

I wrote this book as a manual for the closeted entrepreneur who keeps their innovation abilities suppressed in order to blend into a huge company.

It is premised on three interconnected truths.

1. **The costs of not innovating have never been higher.** New innovative entrants displace entrenched incumbents at an unprecedented rate. There are well-known examples of this, like Blockbuster, Kodak, and Nokia. But on the ground in the Fortune 500, I consistently work with huge companies who are shocked to lose

clients, talent, and market share to new products and new startups. These companies are consistently surprised to learn that their defenses are no longer impregnable. They shouldn't be.

2. **The Wall of Can't.** Despite the threat of disruption, the urgency of innovation always slams into a Wall of Can't. The executives who recognize that innovation is important also simultaneously believe that change is more dangerous than extinction. This miscalculation is reinforced by the managers, stakeholders, and processes that value individual self-preservation over organizational progress. The Wall of Can't in reality is a wall of "won't." And the fallacy of these myths is only exposed when someone breaks them.

3. **The Activated Entrepreneur Underground.** Inside every stale company lies a dormant Entrepreneur Underground. Once they find one another, join together, and act, they can catalyze astounding change.

When that change is catalyzed, it is one of the greatest, most fulfilling moments of entrepreneurial acceleration. It gives a new generation of leaders a voice. It creates a financial New Normal in which growth is measured in multiples rather than percentage points. But we often only see the ribbon-cutting ceremony and not the process. How it works, and who makes it work, is largely a secret.

Until now.

I wrote this book to share the hidden truth of how transformative products are built in conservative companies. I hope that it empowers and emboldens more entrepreneurs to join together and catalyze change for themselves, their customers, and their organizations.

But this book also comes with a warning: it might get you fired.

As scary as that sounds, the only entity I've ever known to regret that decision was the company that had to navigate modernity without the entrepreneurs who can thrive in it.

1

THE INNOVATION THAT'S NECESSARY IS NEVER AUTHORIZED

FIRST CONTACT

In June of 2006, I called Matthew, the CEO of the startup where I worked, Innovest, to offer my resignation.

A day earlier, I had launched my second product ever—and infuriated the biggest banks on Wall Street. I predicted that the booming US housing market would collapse and destroy CountryWide, Bear Stearns, and Lehman Brothers. It was the earliest published prediction of what would later become known as the 2008 financial crisis. But on that day, it felt reckless—not prescient. And it seemed like I had destroyed the startup that had foolishly hired me.

As I waited for Matthew to pick up the phone, my throat tightened. I feared I might cry and humiliate myself even more.

"Greg!" Matthew said jubilantly as he answered the phone. "Or should I call you Nostradamus?"

I thought this was his own sadistic way of firing me. "Matthew, I'm so sorry. I can't believe I put you in this position. I understand fully if you need to fire me."

"What are you talking about? That Bear Stearns is angry?" he asked.

"Everyone's angry, Matthew!"

"Well, is there anything factually incorrect in the report?"

"No, and we've been poring over it all day."

"Good. Well, I've gotten a few stern phone calls today. And I'll tell you what I told them. We are small, but we are not powerless. If any one of them comes after us, I will take out a full-page ad in the *Financial Times* publishing your report and their rebuttal. If they disagree with your opinions but can't discredit your facts, then you're the only one with courage enough to say what you said. Keep going."

"Thank you, Matthew." I felt a warm sense of loyalty and

protection. If we were right, we would enjoy a virtual monopoly on a very big prediction.

We were right. As our forecast came to fruition, our sales skyrocketed. In January 2009, a publicly traded financial services company called RiskMetrics acquired us for $16 million.

Six years and three jobs later, in October 2012, I waited outside of a modern glass boardroom at 8 a.m., wearing a suit for my first-ever meeting with Bloomberg's CEO, Dan Doctoroff. With me were four other members of Bloomberg's innovation team. Jean, a former investment banker, was about to deliver her new product pitch. This product would enable investors to customize stock indexes like the S&P 500 to suit their risk appetite and investment goals.

For a week we had fixated on what not to say to Dan. How to detect ominous shifts in his body language. How not to ignite his volcanic temper. What fonts not to use in our PowerPoint deck. What to include in the catering spread.

Once the meeting began, Jean explained how, in nineteen months, the product she was proposing would hit a revenue inflection point—a 400 percent increase in sales would catapult the software into profitability. She explained how early, enthusiastic market feedback lent credibility to this forecast and that many executives in the organization were already on board.

As she approached her final slide, Dan reached into the middle of the white conference table and helped himself to a muffin from the carefully preselected pastry platter. With food still in his mouth, he finally spoke. "We've been looking for a disruptive product in this market for three years. And this is what we were looking for."

Jean smiled, pressed her hands together, and closed her eyes tightly like she was choking back tears at the Oscars. "Thank you, Dan. We've worked very hard on this."

Like chickens walking toward a fresh bucket of feed, we nodded in relieved, acquiescent unison—even though many of us knew that nobody wanted or needed what she would build with the $8 million that was about to be transferred to her.

The product she was proposing was a replica of a product that my earlier startup, Innovest, had retired six years earlier after two months of no sales. We knew it was going to fail, and we knew we were going to build it anyway. In user tests with Jean's product, people would consistently say, "I don't see how this is different from what I already use." But our deference was critical for our survival. So we said nothing. "It's not like it's our $8 million," we reasoned.

The reason this product would be built and, ultimately, would fail was entirely due to internal corporate politics rather than competitive advantage.

Outside of the conference room, a flat-screen showed that our year-on-year sales were negative for the first time in company history (except for the financial crisis). The first barbarian armies of disruption had finally arrived at our gates. I recognized them because I once was one of them.

THE WALL OF CAN'T

At my startup, Innovest, *disruptive* wasn't a marketing buzzword. It was the blood that coursed through our veins. We had an explicit mandate to force the Wall Street titans who were our competitors to fight us on our own guerrilla terrain. We were wrong often. But when we were right, we enjoyed a virtual monopoly on audacity.

Once I went to work for a huge company, all of that changed.

Everything about a large corporation felt alien. People were afraid to the point of paralysis. They were afraid that someone might get promoted before them. Afraid to challenge their boss's bad idea. Afraid of making a mistake. Afraid of not being invited to the CEO's golf outing. Afraid of building anything without first pitching it in a PowerPoint deck.

These fears resulted in a virtual Wall of Can't.

"We can't build that without outsourcing it to Bangalore."

"We can't talk to that client without permission from Jane."

"We can't build anything before McKinsey crafts a strategy deck."

"We can't, because Mike is fighting with Tom and we'll be seen as siding with Mike."

I considered returning to my startup roots, but frankly, I couldn't afford to. My baby son wasn't getting any smaller, and our rent wasn't getting any cheaper. I needed money and stability that startup life didn't provide.

So I did my best impression of a grown-up. I wore a suit every day. I maxed out my 401(k) contributions. I lost sleep crafting new strategies to get promoted, make more money, get recognized, get respect. I became as deferential and obedient as everyone else. Soon, I made more money than ever before, and I owned a home.

And I hated myself. I had a despondent sense that the world wouldn't notice if I never worked again.

The transition from startup entrepreneur to corporate intrapreneur was the hardest transformation of my professional life. I repeatedly injured myself slamming into the Wall of Can't. But slowly, painfully, I would learn to absorb the impact. I learned to see the obstacles coming and steer around them without losing speed. And eventually, I would learn to create some of the most fulfilling, fast-growing, and impactful products of my career.

I wrote this book to share those lessons. I hope it reaches an intrapreneur who feels as stuck as I did and empowers them to break through their own Wall.

Because once you embrace a certain set of principles and act on them, you will see that the Wall of Can't is quite porous and brittle. It is not driven by inability or impossibility, and certainly not by efficiency. In reality, it is fueled by fear and reinforced by dogma. Corporate intransigence is a choice—it is not a default state.

Breaking through the Wall also entails understanding a core difference between an entrepreneur and an intrapreneur. An entrepreneur has one job: to build a disruptive product and stay disruptive. An intrapreneur has two jobs: they must build a disruptive product and catalyze organizational change. User validation with your market must be reinforced by stakeholder validation internally. Every company is pulled in opposite directions by organizational inertia on one hand and the speed of the disruption economy on the other. This two-pronged problem is the reason why big companies need empowered intrapreneurs. And for an intrapreneur to be effective, they must go to the heart of this tension—forcing a hard choice between embracing change or being eclipsed by it.

This two-pronged mission of product innovation and organizational change is made real when it is reinforced by key principles. I share these principles below, and I elaborate on them throughout the book.

PRINCIPLE 1: INNOVATION ONLY WORKS WHEN IT'S URGENT

Innovation takes root when there's a high cost of not innovating. An intrapreneur can catalyze incredible change only when they focus on a problem that their company must solve but can't solve. Conversely, innovation becomes trivial and isolated when it is not directed toward a mission-critical problem.

This dynamic first became clear to me in 2011, when a wave of populist uprisings known as the Arab Spring created a geopolitical crisis and sent capital markets into a panic. There was no investor playbook for political upheaval like this.

As Bloomberg tried to create a response, my innovation

team was focused on less urgent priorities. But I couldn't stop thinking about it. So, I went to work early on a Saturday and analyzed how oil prices reacted to turmoil in the Middle East for the past forty years. A pattern started to emerge in which prices spiked with the first fever pitch of the news cycle and then retreated, often dropping below their pre-crisis levels.

It was 10 p.m. on a Saturday night by the time I was done, alone in a huge glass skyscraper in midtown Manhattan. I'd been working for fourteen straight hours. And I felt amazing. I'd forgotten how good it felt to solve an important, hard problem. I needed more.

The following Monday, I shared my findings with Ken and Beth, two executives who were trying to build a solution. We'd never met before. They were thrilled that someone had taken the initiative. Later that day, they ran with what I gave them and released it to the market. It became one of the most popular functions on the Bloomberg terminal.

It wasn't a home run. I'd analyzed data in a spreadsheet—I hadn't launched a product. And I hadn't transformed the company. But I had learned a valuable principle for intrapreneurship: a crisis is fertile soil for intrapreneurship to take root. This would prove to be invaluable with later products.

That same product also taught me the second pillar of intrapreneurship: never pitch an idea—always present an outcome. In a huge company, it's easy to say no to an idea. In fact, it's subtly encouraged. Saying no makes an executive seem like a valiant defender of corporate values. It shows that their mental calculator is so seasoned that they can see into the future and calculate risks that no one else has the foresight to see. It makes them look like the thin membrane separating the organization from reckless endangerment.

No one risks anything when they say no to an idea. Which is why a good intrapreneur should never pitch one.

I learned that lesson when my boss Karin got involved after my Arab Spring analysis. She followed protocol and paired me with a team of consultants from McKinsey. For six months, we worked on a business plan for a product that I had already built in one day. The only improvement was that it was wrapped in an ornate thirty-slide PowerPoint deck. Like the Manhattan Project, for six months it was quarantined so no one who needed it could use it. When we finally presented it to the senior leadership team, one of the executives summed up the general mood in the room: "I wish you'd come to us earlier. The Arab Spring was six months ago."

At the same time, a startup called Kensho raised $10 million with a product that analyzed how capital markets would likely react to geopolitical shocks. Today, they're valued at $500 million. Bloomberg had been late and slow, and an upstart had eaten our lunch. That $500 million could have been ours. Incidents like this, when a new entrant would zoom past us while we were tweaking the font for a board presentation, were infuriating. An easily built idea would be overanalyzed, overengineered, and overpoliticized literally to death. As if the world would wait for us to catch up.

That was the last time I would ever present a product before it was already generating results.

PRINCIPLE 3: THE ENTREPRENEUR UNDERGROUND

The intrapreneur who acts alone will be both fired and forgotten. It doesn't matter if their cause is mission critical and their results are indispensable. They'll still be purged. And, in some especially intransigent companies, it will be done publicly to send a warning to others.

It is essential for an intrapreneur to build a coalition. This is one of the hardest and most misunderstood differences between entrepreneurs and intrapreneurs. An entrepreneur in a startup is generally surrounded by like-minded pirates. They usually share a strong sense of mission and drive. They joined a startup because they knew that they were wired a little differently and wanted to find others with the same circuitry.

In a corporation, that's usually not the case. Most people wake up each day hoping to do their job, stay out of trouble, and get home in time for dinner. Additionally, most of the people who are wired like an entrepreneur don't have the terms *innovation*, *intrapreneur*, or *entrepreneur* in their job title. It's hard for intrapreneurs to find one another in a huge company.

The Entrepreneur Underground is a coalition of innovators who find themselves working in a huge company. It is literally the only reason I've ever built anything that mattered. It's also the only reason I didn't go completely insane. For this reason, I devote three chapters to it. In these chapters, I focus on three components of the coalition.

The first component is the Godfather. The Godfather is a powerful executive who is determined to bring the organization into the age of modernity. They have enough authority to neutralize obstructionists, and enough good karma to convert skeptics into supporters. A good Godfather also knows when the resistance you're encountering is reasonable and merits action. The Godfather is the central engine of stakeholder validation.

The second component is the Secret Society. These are

the strategists, developers, designers, thinkers, and doers who are wired to work in a startup but find themselves in a huge company. They are motivated by impact rather than security. When they find one another and work together, they can create momentum that is both unimaginable and unstoppable.

The third component is the Mercenaries. The Mercenaries are the external consultants who do critical work that requires taking risks that can't be taken by someone internal. Mercenaries are like the special forces of enterprise intrapreneurship. They're essential for the success of the mission, but most people can't know that they exist.

PRINCIPLE 4: DON'T SLOW DOWN

When an empowered coalition of intrapreneurs catalyzes critical change, it forces some tough choices about what to do next. These options range from leading a new division or spinning off the product to quitting or getting fired. The right exit is the one where you can sustain your momentum. The intrapreneur's definition of *winning* means building something that solves an entrenched problem better and faster than other incumbent solutions. That definition of victory often diverges from their company's norm, where winning often means more face time with the CEO, more status, more money, and isn't correlated with disruptive product innovation. I devote a chapter to the intrapreneur exit strategy.

PRINCIPLE 5: BUILD IT IN EIGHT WEEKS

These principles are a critical foundation. But they will not change anything until you've built something that has a real impact on people's lives. In 2014, I left Bloomberg. I went on to work with Google, PwC, Viacom, and across the Fortune 500. During that time, I translated these principles into a new, eight-week intrapreneur sprint methodology. During those eight weeks, the principles are translated into a tight cycle of user and stakeholder validation.

In the next chapter, I will share this framework.

11

IF YOU CAN'T LAUNCH IN EIGHT WEEKS, YOU NEVER WILL

OPERATION JEN

Everything would have collapsed if not for Jen.

She enabled PwC to solve a small-business cash flow problem in eight weeks. She enabled my team to break a two-year cycle of false starts and failed launches. She converted a legion of old-guard skeptics into supporters. And the most amazing thing about Jen was that we invented her.

Jen was the human embodiment of cash flow management, an otherwise painfully boring and vast subject.

PwC had tried for two years to launch a small-business cash flow management app when they approached me and my partner agency, Philosophie, to give it one last push. We had eight weeks, and if we failed, they would cut their losses and shut down the project.

The project was PwC's response to an alarming statistic: 70 percent of the small businesses that declare bankruptcy in the US each year are profitable when they fail. Jen was a persona that we developed as the human face of this statistic. She was an independent oil and gas consultant in Texas whose bank account was dwindling even as her sales boomed because her clients started paying her late as oil prices declined.

Creating a cash flow management app would have been an amorphous and insurmountable challenge without Jen. Without her, we would have never gotten past the Wall of Can't. We would have theorized, conceptualized, and analyzed. We would have come up with ideas, concepts, and possibilities. And when we presented them, they would have come across as expensive, risky, and "not the way we do things around here." But after we invented Jen, we found independent consultants that matched her profile and, within days, were testing and validating a prototype with them.

By week five, we had fifty early adopters (one of whom

was actually named Jen). Sixty-three percent of these first users saw their bank balances come back to life. They were able to restructure their debts and payment terms. They gave us leverage with senior leadership. Because of them, we could present an outcome rather than an idea. The executives in PwC who were skeptical started to change their minds once they saw the impact that our product had. Our once-timid executive supporters became more vocal. If our opponents said no now, they'd be letting Jen fail. In eight weeks, an initiative that started with a made-up consultant called Jen, which was slated to be defunded, was granted an additional $2 million.

WHY I WAS RELUCTANT TO WRITE THIS CHAPTER

This chapter is a distilled manual of how I launch new products in eight weeks with huge companies. I was hesitant to write it because in the world of intrapreneurship, there is no such thing as a magic formula. The process that I share here is what has worked for me in a long career of failing and trying again until something durable emerged. But when I work with my clients, at least 50 percent of what we actually do is a response to the events on the ground and the people in the room. If you're dogmatic with this process and don't adapt it to your reality, then you will absolutely fail.

I decided to move forward with this chapter because I

want you to have a set of pragmatic, actionable steps that you can use when you decide to start. I hope that you experiment with it until you can make it work for you.

THE INTRAPRENEUR'S COOKBOOK: THE FIVE STAGES OF AN INTRAPRENEUR SPRINT

In an eight-week intrapreneur sprint, user validation is the engine that drives organizational change. Once you solve an unsolved market problem, you have new power to change your company. Skeptics become zealous converts. Silent supporters become empowered proponents. But that change must be an explicit, strategic goal. It never happens simply because a product is good and change seems like an obvious, good idea. The intrapreneur sprint is different because it recognizes that stakeholder and user validation are deeply intertwined and must be accelerated in tandem.

An intrapreneur sprint works in at least four, and sometimes five stages:

1. Personas: See the world from the perspective of your customer. What's the core problem that they need to solve but can't solve with existing tools?
2. User Journey: How can this customer discover your product, use it to solve a problem, and leave as a loyal evangelist?

3. Fearless Inventory: What assets does your company already have to amplify this product? What deficits prevent your company from doing it? How can you enlist the amplifiers and neutralize the deficits?
4. (Optional) Strategy: How can you differentiate your business model, your product, or your marketing strategy to create an unfair competitive advantage?
5. Release Planning: What can you do to build and test this experience in the first two weeks? How can it be made better in the next two weeks? And made stable in the third and fourth two-week sprints?

Before you start, there are a few people and things you will need:

- One Godfather—You will need one executive ally who is determined to see you succeed and has the clout to enlist other leaders. This is the Godfather. We explore the Godfather further in Chapter 3.
- Two Members of the Secret Society (at least)—These are the designers, developers, and strategists who know how to think, build, and validate like an entrepreneur. We learn more about them in Chapter 4.
- Mercenaries (recommended)—You will likely need to enlist external consultants who are not constrained by your company's rules. We revisit the Mercenaries in Chapter 5.
- The Gatekeepers—In every company, there are law-

yers, compliance managers, and brand managers who decide which products can and cannot get launched. It's best to involve them as early as possible and enlist them as supporters.

- A Product Strategist—This person is like the product's quarterback. They will run the workshops, coordinate the user tests, run the daily and weekly meetings, and manage the whole project.
- Post-it Notes—At least four different colors.
- Colored tape—To convert walls into sprint boards.
- A workflow management system—I use Trello and Jira
- Sharpies—Always use black; otherwise, they aren't legible.
- At least one day (preferably two)—Your team must take at least one day, ideally two, to kick off the new product.
- A room with whiteboards (preferable)—This room should have at least twelve feet of wall space. You should be able to attach Post-it Notes, have meetings, write on whiteboards, and play music (if that's your style) without disturbing others or being interrupted.

That's good enough to get started. Let's go.

STAGE 1: PERSONAS

Too often, companies launch products based on what they want to build rather than what people need. The scope becomes too big, and it's hard to set achievable, actionable goals. The first stage of any new product is to focus on the person who needs you. To do this, the group starts by creating a user persona, like Jen, whom we met earlier. By the time you've completed your persona, your team should have a picture, literally, of your customer. You should have a clear sense of what pain points they're wrestling with and how those affect their life. And you should understand their vision of resolution and success.

Persona development is a four-stage, timed exercise. The first stage is for the product owner to make a two-by-two grid on the wall and to label each section.

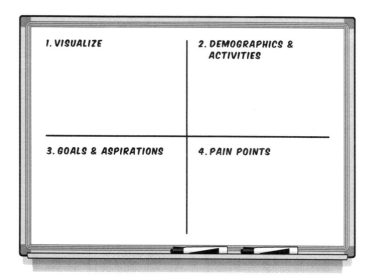

Each person in the group will first complete their own persona by filling in the following sections.

- Visualize (1 minute)—What does your key customer look like? (Draw a picture and give them a name.)
- Demographics and Activities (2 minutes)—what is this person's age, income bracket, gender (if applicable), job description, and any other demographic information that seems relevant?
- Pain Points (3 minutes)—This is the most important section of the persona. What does this person need and not have? How does this unmet need affect their life or job? What is suboptimal about the tools they use today to address this problem?
- Goals and Aspirations (3 minutes)—How can they improve their life? What would success look like? What would entice them to switch to a new product or service?

The product strategist will act as the group's timekeeper. In the "Visualize" section, each person should use one Post-it Note for their picture and name. In each of the other sections, they should write as many ideas as they can and write one idea per Post-it Note. (Everyone should use the same color of Post-it Notes)

When time's up, each person should introduce their persona to the group as they attach their sticky notes to the appropriate section of the persona grid. People will hear that many of their ideas were also written down by others. They should stack overlapping ideas on top of one another so that idea clustering becomes apparent.

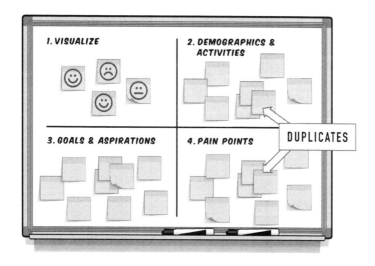

Next, everyone in the group should vote. Each person has two votes to cast in each section. Once everyone votes, you will emerge with a new superpersona. You will have a person with a name and up to five key demographic details, pain points, goals, and aspirations.

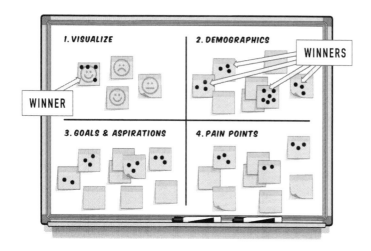

PERSONA VARIATIONS

- **The multipersona product**—Many products have more than one user. This is especially true for business-to-business products where the user, the buyer, and the manager are all different people. For multipersona products, repeat the persona development process for up to four people. Once these personas are developed, you must now vote to select your top-priority users.

- **The empathy map persona**—The four categories that I recommend for persona development (visual, demographics, pain points, and aspirations) are my personal preferences. But there are many good alternatives. One popular alternative is the empathy map. The empathy map uses five categories: thinking, seeing, saying, doing, and feeling. In my experience, this format adds the most value when the goal is a marketing or visual design campaign. It also can help shift the perspective of an engineering team that's having a hard time empathizing with their target customer.

- **Ethnographies**—Many business-to-consumer companies create personas as part of an extensive market research study known as an ethnography. In an ethnography, a company will conduct hundreds of surveys, focus groups, and interviews to form a statistically informed assessment of their target customer. These assessments help determine ad placement, media buying, and other marketing strategies. They're valuable. But they take a long time and are expensive. They may be useful, but you will still need to create your own persona.

- **Stakeholder personas**—In some intrapreneur sprints, it's helpful to identify a key executive swing vote whom you need to enlist as a supporter. What pain points are they wrestling with, and what does success look like for them? It helps you begin to see how serving your user will enable you to win this stakeholder's support.

Now we have the person we will serve.

These personas start to feel real once you start building a product for them. In addition to Jen from Texas, Susan, Enrique, and Todd all appear in my mind as people who moved into my office for a few months. They were like memorable characters from a movie or book. Yet none of them are actual people. I have also launched some products where the name of the persona eventually became the name of the company. (I've been told that this is how Oscar Health Insurance got its name.)

STAGE 2: USER JOURNEY

In the user journey, we will take our persona through the three stages of a new product: entice, engage, and evangelize. The goal of the entice stage is for the customer to find the product and say, "Where have you been all my life?" In the engage stage, the customer should say, "Wow! You can actually solve my problem." And in the evangelize stage, they should say, "I'm coming back with all my friends."

We will begin with an exercise called a storyboard. We will then consolidate everyone's storyboards to create a user journey.

The best way to illustrate this process is to actually create one. So I created a storyboard for a persona called Scot, a twenty-eight-year-old fitness fanatic. Scot's serious about his nutrition and exercise. But he hates the fact that his FitBit, which tracks his physical activity, and his FitnessPal, which tracks his nutrition, don't talk to each other. Every day, he has to become an amateur nutritionist in order to make the right adjustments to his diet or an amateur personal trainer to adjust his exercise to what he ate. We're going to build a tool that solves this problem. We want to enable Scot to adjust his nutrition to respond to his physical activity and vice versa.

We'll start with a storyboard. Each member of the group will set up six Post-it Notes in a row. Think of these Post-it Notes as the six cells of a comic strip. The comic strip will begin with the persona: Scot struggling with a problem. Scot will then discover a new solution, an app, and try it out. The solution will solve his problem. And finally, Scot will introduce other people to the app, restarting the cycle for this other new user. You can use words, draw pictures of the user, draw a social media post, a screenshot of the app, or a meeting with someone who wants to invest a gazillion dollars. Be as creative as you want. (For simplicity's sake, I only used words.)

One person in our group might develop a user journey that looks like this:

Another person in the group might design a user journey that looks like this:

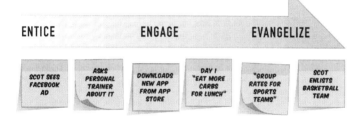

Our job now is to combine these two storyboards. You will need a wall with about six feet of horizontal space for this. Along this wall, the product strategist should place three Post-it Notes, equally spaced to demarcate the *entice*, *engage*, and *evangelize* phases of the user experience. The first member of the group will present their storyboard and place their Post-its under the appropriate heading. The second person will then intersperse their Post-its, depending on the likely sequence of events. Any duplicates should be placed on top of one another. And any steps that would occur concurrently should be stacked vertically. Once everyone in the group presents their storyboards, you will emerge with a more robust, consolidated user journey.

If you're working on a multipersona product or have developed a stakeholder persona, there is one more step. Everyone should create three new Post-It Notes to illustrate where a second user will connect with the first user. (I normally put two minutes on the clock for this step.) Later, these moments of connection will form the basis of a new user journey for the second persona, but not usually until the second eight-week release cycle.

Once everyone's cards are on the board, you have the spine of your new product. More specifically, you have a starting hypothesis of how someone with an entrenched problem would discover your solution, solve their problem with it, and promote it to others.

If we were startup entrepreneurs and not corporate intrapreneurs, we would now move into release planning. We would determine what should be built in the first, second, and third two-week sprints. (We would also create a parking lot for ideas that we may return to someday but can't focus on now.)

But we are intrapreneurs, not entrepreneurs. Before we start release planning, we first must transform our organization.

STAGE 3: THE FEARLESS INVENTORY

An intrapreneur who moves straight into release planning after they've developed their user journey will slam spectacularly into the Wall of Can't. This next stage, the fearless inventory, is where we start to activate the Entrepreneur Underground and focus on organizational change. (On a practical note, make sure to use different-colored Post-it Notes for this section.)

The purpose of the fearless inventory is to assess what your company can and cannot do to solve your user's core problem. There are two layers in this stage: amplifiers and deficits.

Amplifiers are the people, products, technology, and other distinguishing characteristics that make your company able to serve your core user better than anyone else. People tend to first think about technology, brand, or talent when they think of amplifiers. That's a good place to start—but there's room to go deeper. For example, your company may be more profitable than any competitors. Or they may be privately held, while most of their competitors are publicly traded, so they are less exposed to the whims and gyrations of the stock market. Some companies have long-lasting, exclusive relationships with highly coveted clients or suppliers. Amplifiers are the strengths that make it hard for others to compete against you.

Some of these amplifiers may enable you to turn up the volume on a particular feature that was identified in the user journey. (For example, with Scot, we can incorporate machine learning to "listen" to the advice of personal trainers and nutritionists and generate better advice as Scot starts to achieve his fitness goals.) When that's the case, make sure to place that sticky note under the feature it supports and draw an arrow pointing upward to the relevant feature.

The methodology for the amplifiers section follows the same structure as earlier sections. Put three minutes on the clock and ask everyone to write as many amplifiers as they can think of, one amplifier to a Post-it Note. You should emerge from the "Amplifiers" section with an understanding of the people inside of your company whom you need to enlist and the assets that can help you.

Next comes the "Deficits" section. This is a candid assessment of your company's Wall of Can't. It helps identify the causes and costs of not innovating. Who are the people and what are the processes, technologies, or legacy products that stand in the way? It may be helpful to revisit the "Pain Points" section of the persona. Is your organization part of the user's problem? The deficits section is not meant to be bitchy. It is meant to be constructive and honest. You should emerge with a clear assessment of the people and processes that need to be bypassed, converted, or neutralized for you to serve your core customer.

These cards in the Fearless Inventory will translate into the Godfather's roadmap once you get started. It will be their responsibility to enlist and earn the support of key amplifiers and to develop a strategy for addressing the deficits.

By now your wall should look like this:

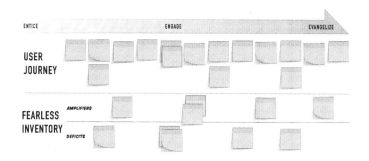

STAGE 4: STRATEGY (OPTIONAL)

Some products need an extra strategy push before the

team is ready to start building, changing lives, and transforming companies. I've developed a fourth, optional differentiation layer that is focused on amplifying the product's competitive advantage. But I don't always use it. Sometimes the persona, user journey, and fearless inventory are enough for a product to solve an entrenched problem in a differentiated way. Sometimes there's also just not enough time to get to it.

In the strategy stage, we focus on eight questions that fall under three headings: business model differentiation, product innovation, and experience differentiation. Please note that no product hits on all eight. A good product will do three of them better than anyone else.

Business Model Differentiation—In this section, we focus on how your business can be structured so that you have an unfair, competitive advantage relative to other solutions. There are two core aspects we focus on: profit model and talent model. (I usually set the timer for three minutes per section.)

- Profit Model—How can we restructure costs or revenue in a way that makes it hard for competitors to emulate our solution? A great example of this is Amazon disrupting brick-and-mortar retailers without owning or renting a single retail outlet. Their profitability on an item sold at a discount is much greater than J.C. Penney, for example, who then has to pay rent on retail space.

- Talent and Organization Structure—How can you enlist and manage talent to drive a competitive advantage? I experienced this at my investment research startup, Innovest. Innovest hired people based on their entrepreneurial skill in a finance industry that primarily drew from the top MBA programs and other banks. We saw financial trends that others could not see because of this.

Product Differentiation—Product differentiation focuses on the features, price, and distribution channels that make the product different.

- Features—Is there a way that the consumer will interact with the product that will make it fundamentally different? The flight-booking app Hopper is an example of this. It ate into the market share of online travel agencies Expedia, Priceline, and Fareportal by allowing the user to set an alert on a flight they were interested in. When the price reaches its lowest likely point, the user receives an alert to book now.
- Price—Is there a way to provide better value for customers? For example, one way Netflix put Blockbuster out of business was by renting movies through a monthly subscription rather than on a transaction basis.

- Distribution Channels—Is there a better way to get your product into the hands of the people who need it? Uber is perhaps the greatest example of this. Before Uber, it was hard to know how to get a cab if you were not in a familiar neighborhood. With their app, anyone who needs a cab can find one—no matter where they are.

Experience Differentiation—This covers areas of customer support, brand differentiation, and community engagement.

- Customer Support—The best example of customer engagement is Zappos. Their customer service teams have total liberty to do whatever it takes to solve a customer's problem. No call scripts.
- Brand Differentiation—A great example of brand differentiation is Oscar Insurance. They recognized that, with the creation of Obamacare, health insurance was now a direct-to-consumer product. Their brand was built on simplicity and accessibility in an industry that is notoriously complex and indecipherable.
- Community Engagement—Harley Davidson is the beacon of community engagement. By owning a Harley, you join a community of Harley owners who meet one another at company-organized rallies. It's more than a bike. Sometimes, this is called a network effect, when a product becomes the connective tissue between a larger group of people.

STAGE 5: RELEASE PLANNING

Now we're ready to start release planning. In this section, we determine what should be the priority in the first two-week sprint, the second, and the third. The fourth sprint is always reserved for presenting your product internally.

To do this, we need another four empty rows.

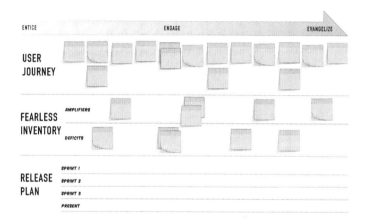

The rule for release planning is as follows: in the first sprint, make the product work; in the second, make it better; in the third, make it stable; and in the fourth, polish the product and present it. In each sprint, there are two levels of tests: user tests and stakeholder tests. User tests are focused on putting your solution in the hands of the user and seeing if it is valuable to them. In a stakeholder test, the Godfather asks other executives who control key assets to support the product.

In each sprint, you should plan to conduct at least ten user tests each week. In these tests, you will test whether your core user can perform a sequence of tasks without any coaching. You will also try to understand whether your solution is valuable to them. These user tests always fail until about week three or four. Don't be discouraged. (We cover this subject in more depth in Chapter 5, "Guerrilla Validation.")

QUANTITATIVE USER VALIDATION

I primarily focus on a kind of qualitative user validation called "usability tests" here, which give you valuable qualitative feedback from ten users in each sprint. For some products, that's not enough. You may need to quantitatively determine if there is demand for your product. You can test this through a landing page test, where you run a social media ad and see how many people click on the ad and offer their email in order to receive a whitepaper or some other giveaway. Another quantitative test is an A/B test. In an A/B test, you run usability tests with two product variants on a large sample of customers and compare which product is more intuitive.

The Godfather will lead at least three stakeholder meetings each week. In the first sprint, these meetings will target people who are likely allies. It is important that the Godfather requests something from each of these stakeholders. These stakeholders may be able to recruit other internal allies, make introductions to key clients who might be early adopters, invest money, share resources, or use their political capital to neutralize opposition that might otherwise derail the project. The Godfather will be able to enlist some key allies because they have a strong, long-standing relationship and can call in a favor. But many of these enlistments will only be possible once certain product milestones are reached. Be clear and specific about which user outcomes are essential for enlisting key stakeholders. Toward the fifth week of the project, when there is a critical mass of user validation, the Godfather should start trying to convert skeptics. This conversion only works in a group setting where there are more enlisted allies than skeptics. We will explore this further in the Godfather chapter.

AGILE 101: WHAT DO YOU DO IN EACH SPRINT?

I strongly suggest that you read one of the great books about agile, like *The Scrum Manifesto* or *The Lean Startup*. But if you don't, here's what you need to know about a sprint. A sprint has at least three phases: sprint planning, user tests, and a retrospective. In sprint planning you focus on what you want to build and test in the current two-week sprint. It is important not to overload a sprint and to only commit to as much as you can realistically achieve. Each of the items you commit to should also be assigned acceptance criteria. These acceptance criteria identify what technical, stakeholder, and/or user tests they must be able to pass in order to be considered done. One day each week should always be set aside to run user tests. And the final day of each sprint should be reserved for a retrospective, where the group gets together and openly discusses what they should start doing, continue doing, and stop doing. I also recommend setting aside a demo day in each sprint once you achieve a strong degree of user validation. During these demo days, you should share footage with key stakeholders of successful user tests.

When you achieve user and stakeholder validation in an eight-week launch, some of the breakthroughs are unexpected.

Our adventure with Jen and the cash flow management app was one of the best examples of this. I mentioned earlier that PwC invested $2 million in the initiative after eight weeks. That's true. But there was a twist. By week seven, our app was accepted in the App Store, and we needed approval from our CEO before we moved forward with the launch.

During the meeting, he and his team were amazed by how much we had achieved in so little time.

One of the executives in the company, Victor, who was opposed to our product, raised a valid question: "Wouldn't this effectively mean that we become a retail software developer rather than the enterprise consultancy that we already are? Isn't this a distraction from where we need to go?"

The CEO thought about it for a few seconds, turned to Victor, and said, "That's an excellent point, Victor."

He then turned to us and announced, "Guys, we will pay you $2 million to not launch this. Victor's business is in a heap of shit. I'd rather invest in you taking another eight weeks to rescue his $76 million shitshow than dicking around in the App Store."

Victor's cost of not innovating was $76 million. Once the CEO realized that he had a team that could reverse the tide of stagnation, the question was where to aim the rocket and how to add fuel.

We created a choice between stagnation and acceleration. Obstacles that previously seemed entrenched and insurmountable now seemed bite-size.

It started with Jen, and it took eight weeks.

III

—

THE GODFATHER

TWO GUYS LAUNCH A PRODUCT WITH APPLE...

In 2014 Apple secretly prepared to launch a new wearable mobile device: the Apple Watch. They invited thirteen companies to send their top designers to Apple's headquarters to develop apps that would be featured by Apple's CEO, Tim Cook, at the launch event. One of those companies was Starwood Hotels, which sent Stephen Gates. Another was a telecommunications giant (who shall remain anonymous for soon-to-be-obvious reasons), which sent Adam.

Adam and Stephen have a lot in common. Both their parents were designers. Both only wear jeans and black shirts. (For formal occasions they wear black jeans.) They pulsate with energy when they get excited. And like most lifelong designers, flying out to Cupertino to design for an Apple product launch was the fulfillment of a lifelong dream.

But it would end very differently for each of them.

Stephen joined Starwood after serving as creative director with companies like ExxonMobil, Sprint, and American Airlines. He arrived at Starwood at the same time as its new CEO, Fritz Van Paaschen, who embraced Stephen as an important agent of organizational change and innovation. Stephen's team was in the middle of an intense release cycle when the invitation came from Apple.

Four people in Starwood were allowed to know where Stephen was while he was working with Apple. "Our Chief Marketing Officer found out what I had been doing when he saw Tim Cook presenting the Starwood app on the day the Apple Watch was launched," Stephen explained to me. For three months, at midnight East Coast time and 9 p.m. in California, Stephen would brief his CEO, Fritz Van Paaschen. "Fritz very deliberately protected me from the day-to-day operations of Starwood that I would normally oversee so that I could focus on fulfilling this dream." It was an incredible demonstration of trust and loyalty.

Stephen developed an Apple Watch app that could unlock your hotel room, remember your room number, and provide quick-glance details about your stay. He returned home to Starwood a hero, and the app was showcased onstage by Tim Cook when Apple launched the watch.

Unlike Stephen's triumph, Adam's trip to Cupertino ended in failure.

Adam joined his company when they acquired his startup. which built one of the first smartphone applications that could stream video from a home security camera. The telecommunications giant had spent years trying to build something similar but couldn't catch up to his startup. After the acquisition the leadership team that used to compete against Adam before he was acquired felt threatened by him. All of the acceleration he had catalyzed in his startup quickly ground to a halt. When the call came for Adam to fly out to Apple's headquarters, he was locked in a costly political stalemate with executives who were determined to see him fail.

But despite the political acrimony, on the flight to California, Adam was infused with an intense and focused calm. "I'm designing a product for an Apple launch." He repeated this to himself like a Buddhist chant. This was the dream.

When he arrived at Apple's headquarters, he created an app that could stream live video from a home security camera on a watch. Apple loved it. They were amazed that live-streaming video could be accessed on a device as small as a watch. They loved how, in user tests, people knew exactly what they were seeing and what they were supposed to do next. They loved that something so advanced was so simple.

But Apple's excitement only made it more urgent for his internal rivals at his company to stop him. When he came back to Atlanta from Cupertino, he was summoned to a meeting with the company's executives, where he was reprimanded. "We never authorized you to develop video," they said. "It's against our cyber-security protocol." Adam knew that this was a bullshit excuse; he had worked with a developer who ensured that it was compatible with their security guidelines. But his rivals found a new excuse. "It will be too much of a surprise to our customers."

His company would only authorize him to build an app that could arm and disarm a home security system. The live-streaming video was cut. Apple was as disappointed as Adam was. Both of them were furious that the problem wasn't technical ability or even security constraints. It was politics. Apple thanked Adam for his time and ended the collaboration with his company.

Stephen Gates succeeded because he had a Godfather; his CEO supported and protected him so that he could capitalize on an extraordinary opportunity.

Adam failed because he was forced to fend for himself

against an executive team that was politically motivated to thwart him.

THE BRICKS IN THE WALL OF CAN'T

The Godfather is the one executive who is more afraid of extinction than change. They have a long, powerful legacy in the organization and are determined to use this power to fuel an innovation transformation. They are an essential component of the Entrepreneur Underground. The Wall of Can't is indecipherable and insurmountable without them.

To understand how critical the Godfather is, it is important to delve a little deeper into the Wall of Can't.

When someone in a big company says, "I can't," it's hard to know what they really mean.

Sometimes they say, "I can't," because what you're asking them to do is impossible. They lack the technology, people, money, or knowledge to perform the task that you've asked of them. They can't because they are unable.

Other times "can't" means that they can do it but see unintended consequences that could be fatal. They have the ability to do it. But you might damage the company's brand, profitability, or good standing with regulators.

They can, but they shouldn't. At least not before risk is re-assesses or someone more senior says it's okay.

But just as often, "can't" is just a bullshit excuse for "won't," "I would prefer not to," or "I don't see how this will make me look good." It is driven by myopic politics. It is a crutch for someone who is worried that you will look better than they will. Or that they will become obsolete if you succeed. Or they are jealous that you will have more face time with the CEO. In other words, they can, but they don't see how it will advance their self-interest, so they won't—even if the project is mission critical. When this "can't" paradigm becomes the norm, the costs of not innovating skyrocket. Huge piles of money get left on the table so that someone can pursue something as minor as a small raise or be invited to a golf outing with the CEO. This subspecies of "can't" is why Adam was thwarted and is why his company was absent from the launch of the Apple Watch.

The true underlying cause of "can't" is indecipherable without an executive who has encountered all forms of resistance before. Such an executive will know precisely when and how to say, "You can. You should. And you will." And this executive will be able to enlist the support of other executives.

That executive is the Godfather. They are determined to

use their power to leave a legacy of innovation and progress. They are the ladder that enables the intrapreneur to scale the Wall of Can't.

"KILL ME FIRST." THE MAKINGS OF A GODFATHER

The value of a Godfather is realized only once things start to go badly. When technology breaks, sales plummet, users don't respond, and a small army of opponents takes screenshots to support their case that you should be publicly executed. Those moments are harrowing because you're never totally innocent. There is merit to the argument that there is an established system where none of these growing pains are a problem. That is rarely the full motivation for the assault. But it's the part that's hard to defend against.

That's when you need a Godfather—when you won't survive unless someone powerful steps forward and says, "Kill me first."

Loyalty under fire is ultimately what differentiates a Godfather from a typical sponsor. A sponsor may invest money, share resources, introduce you to the CEO, or introduce you to clients. But a sponsor is just betting on you—they're not going to bat for you. They bail out as soon as there's any turbulence. The Godfather fights through turbulence.

In addition to loyalty under pressure, a good Godfather possesses some other important traits:

- **A track record of launching new businesses**—Many great Godfathers have a track record of launching new businesses and fixing failed ones. This usually means that they have experience navigating the constraints and obstructions that any new intrapreneurial venture will need to overcome. It also means that, if those businesses are still viable, there is a large group of people who owe their career to the Godfather. They emerge from these endeavors with a coalition of allies and a keen understanding of where the obstacles are hidden.
- **Startup roots (sometimes)**—An executive with startup roots is either a huge asset or a fatal liability as a Godfather. Some startup CEOs thrive post acquisition. They infuse the organization with the entrepreneurial spirit that underpinned their success as an entrepreneur. They build trust with the CEO and executive leadership team, and they create a financial and innovation inflection point that was badly needed.

That's the utopian scenario. Sometimes it comes true.

My startup's COO thrived after we were acquired. He rediscovered his passion for building something he loved once the weight of making payroll and dealing with irate clients was someone else's job. He became a mentor to many other intrapreneurs in the company and became a Godfather for many product teams.

Our CEO, on the other hand, imploded after we were acquired. Gone was the driven, high-energy visionary who rallied his troops through the epicenter of certain-death storms. In his place was an angry, aggrieved, exhausted cynic who wished nothing but total destruction on the company that constrained him with rules and supervisors. He was a great CEO—but a horrible intrapreneur and an even worse Godfather.

I've been through seven acquisitions since then. Most startup CEOs incinerate after they get acquired and are horrible Godfathers. But those who thrive tend to be outstanding.

THE STAKEHOLDER PERSONA

The primary responsibility of the Godfather is enlisting other executive supporters.

Their primary instinct normally will be to draw up a list of names of other stakeholders they want to enlist as supporters and then begin to meet with them. But in my experience, they need to be more methodical about this. That's why I created the stakeholder persona.

The stakeholder persona follows the same format as the user persona. It helps to identify other powerful people in the organization who need things to change.

Once the persona is developed, it is important to then draw up a list of key early allies. It's also important to identify key market and user outcomes that will help enlist them.

NAME AND SKETCH

PERSONAL AMBITIONS:	RESPONSIBILITIES:
GOALS FOR THE COMPANY:	FEARS:
ALLIES AND ASSETS:	THREATS:

HOW TO FIND A GOOD GODFATHER

Godfathering is not for the fainthearted, so it should not be easy for a Godfather to say yes when you ask for their support. You need to have a direct, candid conversation about the risks you're prepared to take, the processes and people you're prepared to challenge, and the magnitude of what could go wrong.

For example, one of the greatest Godfathers I ever worked with was Dave. I was still reeling from a spate of intense political warfare that had destroyed a product that should have been a huge success. When I met Dave, I was excited about the product that Dave wanted me to help build, but I didn't have the stomach for another round of political gridlock.

During our first meeting, I was leaning toward saying no. "Dave, what excites me about this product is that it takes a service that has historically been accessible to a small cadre of corporate executives and makes it available to everyone who needs it," I said. "It illuminates a problem that is obvious to everyone as soon as you point it out.

"What terrifies me is that there are literally thousands of people in your own company who would have to fight to keep their jobs if this ever took off. I just quit a job where everyone with power tried to kill me and no one would defend me. I don't want to go through that again."

Dave smiled and responded, "There's no doubt that we are the digital camera lab within Kodak. They'll definitely come after us. But they can't afford for us not to win. That's why this is fun. Who cares if we all lose our jobs? I've been launching businesses here for thirty years, and all the good ones infuriated lots of people."

Every intrapreneur I've ever known who had a great Godfather can point to some version of the same conversation in which they had a candid talk about the risks and consequences of what lay ahead.

THE LOGICAL NEXT STEP VS. THE COLD CALL

Some Godfather-intrapreneur partnerships emerge from a long-standing relationship. Others occur because someone had the courage to introduce themselves to a stranger.

After a while, in any company, you find senior leaders whose ambitions, strengths, and frustrations are aligned with your own. You will become friends. And eventually it will make sense for you to work on a project together. It is the intrapreneur's responsibility to be very clear that this is an eight-week sprint and not just another project. But the formality of enlisting the Godfather seems like an organic outgrowth of an existing relationship.

Other Godfather-intrapreneur partnerships start simply

because someone introduces themselves. If you have a strong sense that a serious problem will spiral of control if the organization can't retain and empower you, then you should say so. Find the executive who you think is most likely to listen and tell them. Or send a note directly to your CEO.

The most legendary example of this is when Steve Jobs returned to Apple and met Jony Ive. Jony was a frustrated designer who felt stifled by the suffocating bureaucracy that engulfed Apple after Jobs left. He brought a copy of his resignation letter to their first meeting. But once he and Steve Jobs started to go through his designs, things quickly changed. They recognized one another as kindred spirits. Ive wound up designing the iMac, which became a bestseller for Apple. He remains Apple's head of design.

The most important thing is to present an outcome to the Godfather rather than an idea. Their level of commitment when they see a solution beginning to take form is always greater than their response to a concept. Also, without a solution, it may seem like your common ground is frustration with the status quo rather than a commitment to change it. Saying, "We have an opportunity to solve an entrenched problem in a differentiated way," is always more compelling than, "Doesn't this suck?"

An intrapreneur without a Godfather has a very low probability of success and a high probability of stagnation. All progress in terms of user and market validation will likely be negated by unaddressed organizational debt. This doesn't necessarily mean that you should quit. But you should be realistic about what you can achieve. Your best hope may be to operate in stealth mode, set a low bar for user and market validation, and use these results to enlist a Godfather.

It may also be that your best hope is to leave. When Adam went back to work at his telecommunications company, it was clear that he could be more impactful elsewhere. In the past, the near-term financial stability that he enjoyed enabled him to endure his slow progress. But after Apple, he could no longer justify it. He felt like he was wasting his talent. He quit. And like most intrapreneurs I've ever met who did the same thing, he's now doing the best work of his life and making more money than at any other point in his career.

IV

THE SECRET SOCIETY

The purpose of the war display was to avoid war.

Like the New Zealand tribal war dance, the haka, the movements, shapes, and colors were intended to project omnipotence.

The Apex Predators wore Ferragamo. The soldiers beneath them wore Hermès. Beneath them, you would see Yves Saint Laurent and Canali. After that came Thomas Pink. Then you had the hired help, who wore whatever designer labels were on sale.

Occasionally, the Elder Apex Predator would dress as hired help. He would wear a shirt with stains under the armpits and an outdated tie. "Even though I've been here a long time, I'm still approachable," the gesture conveyed. "But know that my status is self-evident."

I ventured out onto my big bank's Upper East Side balcony on a summer Thursday to catch my breath and have a coffee in the middle of an intense product sprint that was going very badly. A twenty-something who appeared to be a recent MBA graduate held the door for me, wearing an out-of-caste Ferragamo tie. "Either he works in the CEO's office, or he's about to get killed," I thought.

I sat on a midcentury, modern picnic bench, sipped my coffee, and was unwrapping a sandwich when something made me notice that it was beautiful outside.

A man wearing a plain T-shirt and jeans was painting a still life of a vase of flowers. The posturing of the war display vanished as he dipped a small brush into a watercolor tray.

"I hope I'm not crashing your party," I said, "but your painting just reminded me that it's beautiful outside and that I should take time to notice." I had to share how he had made me feel.

"Thanks!" He smiled. "It makes me feel good, too."

"I almost did my undergrad in fine art," I said.

"I would never have guessed that from looking at you." He smiled and jerked his chin at my clothes.

I was wearing a dark-blue pinstriped suit, a stiff white dress shirt, and no tie.

"This isn't who I am. It's just the suit that I wear to work."

Unlike me, Hansel Perez actually persevered with a degree in art and eventually shifted into graphic design. He graduated into the epicenter of the first dot-com boom and fell in love with the burgeoning field of user experience design.

When I met him on the porch, he was one of Bloomberg's most senior designers. I felt like I knew him already, and wished I'd met him earlier.

What I loved about Hansel was that once I met him I didn't feel alone anymore. We got each other. We had both experienced the magic moment when a product finally connects with its target user, and we immediately knew that we'd spend the rest of our careers chasing that high. And yet we found ourselves here. Unlike me, he loved it. "Empathy at scale," he used to say. He loved working on products where, if he got it right, the results could be amplified on an incredible scale.

Through Hansel, I was looped into an innovation underground within Bloomberg of designers, geeks, thinkers, and doers who saw me as a like-minded soul. They didn't put their innovative ambitions on hold once they joined the company. They were all nice—if you met them, you'd think they were friendly, respectful, and approachable—but their creative drive wasn't up for negotiation. Once we found one another, we felt empowered and emboldened to make that clear from the outset.

I don't think I ever explicitly asked Hansel to lead design on my next three products. I simply explained what I was working on, and a week later, we were kicking off an eight-week sprint.

I don't recall Hansel asking me to run product strategy for his two biggest products. He didn't have to. I saw that he needed a product strategist, and I did it.

PRESSURE VS. STRESS

What seems remarkable in retrospect is that our first two products together were totally covert. We helped each other on nights and weekends. We worked ninety hours a week and didn't notice. It felt so fucking good to feel some high-velocity wind in my hair that I didn't notice what time it was.

I've always said that stress = pressure × drama. Pressure is healthy—stress is not. The fifty-hour weeks that I had to endure doing bullshit work took a much bigger toll than the ninety-hour weeks building something invigorating. The Entrapreneur Underground was the only way we could keep our work from veering into the wrong lane. It helped us stay in the pressure zone and avoid the stress zone.

PUNKS AND PINSTRIPES

A great intrapreneur team is a strange cocktail of people who don't seem like they belong together. And once you join this Secret Society, you realize the people who seek entry are not who you'd expect.

Stephen Gates, the global head of design at Citigroup (also the creator of the amazing podcast *The Crazy One*), told me the greatest secret society story of them all.

It happened when he was the design director for Starwood and was invited by Apple to participate in a design sprint for a new product (described in an Chapter 3).

When he flew home, the contrast between the energy in Apple's product lab and his routine at Starwood was tough to endure. "I felt like I was falling down as a leader," he said. "I wasn't creating enough creative moments."

He knew he needed to change.

He started by changing the format of his weekly design

meeting. When he began at Starwood, the weekly design roundup was primarily a checkup on all the projects that were in flight. It was more transactional than it was empathetic. He changed the format so that one person would share a ten-minute personal narrative on what inspired them and how it infused their work. Then the entire group would share. The meeting refreshed each sprint with deep, human interconnectedness.

He also opened the meeting so that anyone in the company was welcome to join. Soon, his conference room overflowed with lawyers, finance directors, designers, and developers eager to listen, engage, and share stories about inspiration. The energy of these meetings slowly started to infuse the culture of the entire organization.

THE DREAM INTRAPRENEUR

The ideal intrapreneur team is bonded by a sense of punk rock solidarity that can be hard to find in a big company. Many intrapreneurs stumble right out of the gate because they underestimate the value of people who feel solidarity and loyalty to the mission.

Intrapreneurs possess three core characteristics:

- Punk—They are willing to break unnecessary rules in a way that emboldens and motivates others.

- Compassion—They're nice. Candor and subversiveness should not be mistaken to mean "acts like an asshole." They are the kind of person whom others want to work with.
- Resourcefulness—They use whatever's available to accelerate change, often in a way that reinvents a process that is entrenched and inefficient. Ideally, they are (or can recruit) a full-stack designer (someone who can design a product directly into code) so that a website or app is shippable for testing as soon as it's conceptualized.

Jake was one of the greatest intrapreneurs I've ever worked with. Jake's hair fell down to his shoulders, and he wore sneakers, tattered T-shirts, and jeans to work every day in an investment bank where everyone else wore a custom-tailored suit. He began his relationship with the firm as an external software consultant. His main client was later promoted to senior partner and extended an offer to Jake to join him as a full-time employee rather than an external consultant. "Sure," Jake said. "But I'm not changing my clothes."

Jake was unusually adept at managing huge projects, like a $100 million acquisition, and launching new, innovative products. He had an innate sense of the ulterior motives that executives were calculating when they considered a new project. He also was just nice. He remembered birthdays. He would ask someone if their kids got off to college okay. He would buy people books if he thought they would enjoy them. Many conservative executives who were initially put off by his attire came to embrace him as a breath of fresh air. He also looked so different that he inadvertently acted as a living billboard, inviting the closeted intrapreneurs in the organization to introduce themselves.

COMMON CHARACTERISTICS OF THE ENTREPRENEUR UNDERGROUND
STARTUP ROOTS

Many great intrapreneurs came to a huge company after some time in a startup. They have a clear sense of what it's like to launch with and without corporate constraints. They invariably have identified bottlenecks in the organization's culture and processes that stand in the way of innovation. And they have a clear sense of how to achieve user and market validation without bureaucracy.

Their reasons for leaving the startup world are an important litmus test. Many will have been with companies that were acquired by the enterprise or will have entered a phase in life where startup volatility and risk is not sustainable. These are great origin stories of great intrapreneurs. But others will have fled from a startup to the enterprise because they craved the stability and linearity of a huge company. These startup expats usually make bad intrapreneurs.

THEY'RE WEIRD

Most great intrapreneurs I know are unapologetically different from everyone else. They have weird hobbies like rice calligraphy or spelunking. Like Hansel, they duck out for a few minutes during lunch and paint still lifes of flowers. A disproportionate number of them love punk music and have played in punk bands. Someone who works in the enterprise and loves Patti Smith shows lots of promise.

ESCAPE VELOCITY

Very few people in the enterprise know what it feels like to work at the speed of startups. It's critical to have a team that knows what that kind of momentum and speed feel like. The Secret Society knows how quickly a startup trying to put your company out of business could move and knows what it feels like to operate at that same speed.

THE ENDURING IMPACT OF THE ENTREPRENEUR UNDERGROUND

I literally owe my entire career to the Secret Society. When I knew I needed to quit Bloomberg, I had to reconcile with the economic reality of having two small kids and a mortgage. Hansel and I went out for a drink, and I explained to him how I was terrified about the risk I knew I needed to take. I was in bad shape. My wife, my dad, and my brother all thought I should stay in my job until I found a new one. I wasn't eating or sleeping or really living well in any way.

I got up to go to the bathroom. When I came back, Hansel was smiling. "Guess what!" he grinned.

"What?"

"I just texted my friend Dan, who's looking for a product strategist to help him on a major project with Viacom. He knew your work when he was at Bloomberg. He wants to hire you if you're ready to quit."

Literally, every client I've ever worked for was referred to me by the Secret Society. The karma bank account of the Entrapreneur Underground pays dividends that are different than just normal colleagues. They don't simply help you build products. They empower you to be your truest self. They connect you into a mostly invisible power grid of innovation and support.

It stays with you.

V

—

GUERRILLA VALIDATION

Once you drive east of Cooper Park in Brooklyn, the landscape changes to what Brooklyn looked like when I was a kid in the eighties. Blocks of brick townhouses, glass luxury apartments, and hipster coffee shops give way to abandoned skeletons of industrial warehouses. Clouds of diesel blacken the air. Huge corrugated steel warehouses rattle and clang when the wind blows. There are no food trucks selling designer Korean tacos. The food trucks here sell hot dogs, potato chips, and soda— that's it.

I picked up my two developers, Brooke and Aliya, from a hipster coffee shop to bring them to a user test at a concrete plant in east Brooklyn. We drove past the ruins of what used to be the Greenpoint Hospital, past my Uncle James's steel factory, and into a parking space that was clearly reserved for a concrete mixer.

Men in hard hats and industrial overalls nodded their heads in an old-school, wordless greeting at Brooke and Aliya in their skinny jeans and vintage sweaters. They had each lived in Brooklyn for three years and had never met people who used the term *yous* as the second-person, plural pronoun. Until now.

Gary came out, shook my hand with his right hand, and slap-hugged my back with his left hand. "How ya doin' Greg?" He then smiled politely at Brooke and Aliya, "How ya doin', ladies? Can I offer yous a soda or a cawfee?"

Gary was a dispatcher for Empire Concrete, the largest concrete company in New York City. We had been hired by Google to develop a software prototype for industrial service companies. We had developed a few concepts and were ready to test them. But we hit a snag. The executives who had warm relationships with companies like AT&T, ExxonMobil, and DirecTV were reluctant to introduce us to those brand-name clients. And frankly, I didn't blame them. We were total amateurs armed with a perfunctory hypothesis about what the industry needed and didn't have. I can understand why they wanted some degree of validation before they vouched for us.

But with or without them, we still needed to test our software. So I resorted to stalking. For two weeks, I was out the door at dawn, driving to truck stops in the Bronx and the outer reaches of Brooklyn and Queens. I approached drivers as they climbed out of their cabs to have a cigarette and refuel, asking them if they would participate in a software user test for $200. I tailed cement mixers and fuel trucks as they wound down side streets and pulled into their depots. I revived my New York accent, which I had as a kid growing up in Queens but have since mostly lost. We eventually recruited a few drivers and dispatchers. But we needed to test it with a company. So I finally asked my Uncle James, who runs a steel plant, to introduce me to his friends at Empire Concrete, which led me to Gary Ortiz.

We had developed a software prototype to help dispatchers like Gary work more effectively with the workers who spend their days in the field. Our goal for this meeting was to see if Gary could perform a series of tasks in our software with no coaching and to test if the value proposition was compelling.

I set up a video camera to film the test while Brooke and Aliya set up their laptops so that Gary could start. That's when the real problem that we needed to solve jumped out at us.

Gary's walkie-talkie crackled. "GARY! Where da' fuck did you send us this morning? The guys at Pinnacle Construction are pissed off!"

Gary nodded at Brooke and Aliya and said, "Gimme a

second. I gotta deal wit dis." He then picked up his walkie talkie and with counterintuitive calm said, "Copy, Mike. I'll deal with it."

The walkie talkie crackled back, "Ten four."

Gary turned back to Brooke and Aliya. "Sorry 'bout dat. Yous ready?"

Aliya responded with a question. "How often does that happen?"

"When the union is getting ready to renegotiate their contracts—every day." Gary explained to us that he was in the middle of a perennial battle with his drivers' union. This battle occurred every January when their contracts were set to be renegotiated. The drivers, Gary explained, would find any excuse to cry foul: Gary gave them bad instructions, botched the order, sent the wrong guys out to the job. This was all part of a negotiating strategy, Gary believed, to claim duress during contract negotiations.

"Is there any chance we can talk to that driver or another driver after this?"

"As long as you pay them, sure."

All of the software that Gary had in his dispatch room

was like industrial babysitting equipment. Alarms would go off if a driver was late, if a driver was taking too long at a rest stop, if a driver took a wrong turn. The starting premise for all of this software seemed to be, "We'll help you win the war against your workforce." No wonder the union wanted to kill him.

In every product, there is the stated problem, and then there's the real problem. This was the real problem. Their software systems discouraged collaboration and trust.

But when we drove around with Mike and some of the other drivers, we saw something different from what Gary saw. All the same buzzes and beeps that went off in Gary's office went off on his workers' mobile devices. Their software made it seem as though they were running a network of meth labs from the back of their concrete mixers.

But the unseen truth was that they spent most of their time helping one another.

A week after our first session with Gary and Mike, we were ready to test a new solution. We started with Mike and four other drivers.

The concrete in one of their trucks was starting to dry before it was poured. Mike, the driver, was stuck in traffic and was concerned that by the time he arrived at the site, it would be too dry to use. After ten minutes, a push notification appeared on his phone. "We're here to help. Let us know if you're stuck."

When Mike got that message, he did something I had never seen him do before. He smiled.

He then pressed a button that alerted four of his colleagues that he needed help. His iPhone knew that he was driving and couldn't text. Soon his phone rang. "Hi, Mike, I saw that you were stuck. What's up?"

The other driver told Mike about a valve that he could close in order to prevent moisture from escaping. Then he needed to add some water when he arrived at the site. Crisis averted.

That was the first installment of our solution.

As we rolled out this solution to more people within the company, incredible results started to materialize. On-time completion rates shot up by 43 percent. Gary's walkie talkie ceased to crackle with veiled threats of labor unrest. And they were able to increase the number of jobs to be done in a day, which increased quarterly sales by 24 percent.

Moments like these are the part of my job that gives me

the greatest joy. When you create something as simple as a push notification and it changes how a person experiences their job, and creates an inflection point for their company and industry. I get to be present at the birth of these ideas and also to help raise them into fully formed solutions in a matter of weeks.

It's counterintuitive, but building software can be one of the most intimate forms of human connectivity. When you do it right, you can see the world through the eyes of the person you're trying to serve. You gain a very precise sense of what oar needs to be placed in the water to change the direction of their life.

YOU'RE EXPENDABLE UNTIL YOU'RE FAST

Guerrilla validation is essential for conveying a sense of urgency in the enterprise. When you're releasing new products in a two-week cadence in a company that typically doesn't move that fast, it creates a sense of unstoppable inevitability about your product. Once your target market starts to respond, the difference between what your customers need and what your company provides falls into stark contrast.

Senior executives in a major company tend to believe that they completely know their customer and are doing a great job—even when they're not. An intrapreneur trying to solve an entrenched problem better than a large company's existing solution will often be told, "I've been working in this business for twenty-five years." As if tenure is an adequate substitute for empathy and understanding.

Too many intrapreneurs respond to this challenge by crafting their retort of why their insight into the customer is more accurate. They shouldn't. It is an unwinnable argument and a dangerous trap.

Guerrilla validation enables customers to speak for themselves.

There are two stages to guerrilla validation: user experience validation and A/B testing. I'll quickly explain both. (I also encourage you to read two outstanding books on the subject. *A/B Testing* by Dan Siroker and Pete Koomen, and *Lean UX* by Jeff Gothelf and Josh Seiden)

The first user tests of a product should begin five days after kickoff and should be followed by at least ten user tests each week afterwards.

USER TESTING 101

1. Ask them no more than ten questions to gauge:

- How does the problem you want to solve manifest itself for them?
- How often does it occur?
- How do they try to solve the problem now?
- When did they have a successful experience resolving it? What happened?
- When did they have a bad experience?

2. Ask them to perform a series of tasks with your prototype. Explain that you would like them to think out loud as they navigate from screen to screen.

3. At each screen, ask three questions:

- What do you think you're supposed to accomplish with this screen?
- What action do you think you're supposed to take to accomplish it?
- What do you expect will happen once you take that action?

4. Once they complete all of the tasks and have taken a round trip tour of the product, ask some concluding questions:

- If this product were a person, how would you describe them?
- Would you trust this person?
- How would you try to convince a friend to use this product or convince your boss to buy it?

"User acceptance" occurs when the user knows exactly what to do in each screen and understands the value of each interaction with the product. If at any time you need to explain how to complete a task, if the user doesn't see value in the product, or if they don't describe the product as important to use or own to someone else, then you've learned how to improve the product.

When you are simulating a product that would require multiple users to use it at the same time (for example, the dispatcher app that I described in the beginning of this chapter), then the different users should sit in separate rooms while the people conducting the test communicate through phone or text to signal when one user has completed an action that should trigger a new action for the other user.

Once the design has been built into working software, then none of these simulations are necessary anymore. You can conduct user tests with a real app being used in its natural habitat.

I have probably conducted a thousand user tests in my life, and the first round is always a failure. Always. Nobody knows what button to press, they struggle to understand the value proposition that we hoped would resonate. In addition, what I almost always experience is that cutting-edge technology, like AI, virtual reality, and the blockchain, that is supposed to transform the world, is almost always met with utter indifference by users. "But that screen was powered by artificial intelligence," we want to plead with them. They don't give a shit. This, too, is valuable learning. It prevents software developers from investing scarce resources in nascent technology that hasn't yet found a real market need.

These first missteps are incredibly powerful. In effect, your target user shows you exactly how to refine and optimize the product so that they can buy it from you. Invalidation badly bruises the ego, but it's the only way to make your product better. You will notice that a button is clear in one screen but hard to find in another. That one interaction is buggy and that people start to drop out of the app. It sucks to see people struggle with your creation, but these data points become the product. You learn what's right only once you build something that's wrong.

A product and/or feature is ready once nine out of ten users can complete an uncoached round-trip tour of the solution and can accurately explain its value to someone else.

Then the next stage kicks in, which is A/B testing. In an A/B test, you take two different versions of the same product that have already achieved user acceptance and test them against one another. (As I write this chapter, I am currently running a series of A/B tests for a huge online travel agency. Every day, we track how long it takes one hundred visitors to choose their flight and reach the payments page on two different versions of the website. Once we run a thousand tests, the highest speed user flow wins.)

GUERRILLA VALIDATION ILLUMINATES THE COST OF NOT INNOVATING— AND PEOPLE WILL HATE YOU FOR IT

The incredible power of guerilla validation is speed. In an eight-week release cycle, you can reasonably expect to achieve 90 percent user acceptance around week three or four. That kind of velocity stands in stark contrast to a large company that operates in monthly, quarterly, or even annual strategic planning cycles. High velocity validation enables an intrapreneur to convey how quickly an outside team could come out of nowhere and start stealing customers. Once you achieve it you become indispensable because you'd be a much bigger threat if you achieved it outside of the organization.

That's when you will get into serious trouble from everyone who believes they're already doing it right.

People in big companies fight guerrilla validation for three reasons:

- They're afraid of failure
- They're afraid of losing power
- You're genuinely wrong

1. Fear of failure—The fact that guerrilla validation always fails in the first few weeks will often be cited as evidence that you are out of your depth and should let the grown-ups drive. For a company with an established product and a predictable revenue stream, innovation will often seem like a reckless diversion of resources from something which is good enough to something which isn't. You will be told that you're damaging the company's reputation and wasting its money. And if you're not addressing a problem with a high cost of not innovating—then you will not be able to defend yourself against this argument. You will likely not have enough political protection and time to achieve meaningful user acceptance.

2. Fear of losing power—Good guerrilla validation will often mean that you demonstrate that someone who is very powerful doesn't deserve to be. Their product, their customer service, and their speed may all be exposed as antiquated and suboptimal. This becomes especially pronounced in business-to-business companies where the customer is another huge company. The people who own these corporate relationships guard them with their lives. Very often, they will not voluntarily introduce you to their clients so that you can test your new product—even if their clients may need it. There are only two strategies in these scenarios. The first is to develop a relationship of your own with the customer and, once you achieve user acceptance, to ask the relationship manager to help

you accelerate it. Or go over their head. If the cost of not innovating is high enough, then you should receive support from your Godfather or CEO.

This fuels a huge clash of titans, which is both necessary and scary.

The only time I've ever seen an executive get physically violent in my career was in such a scenario. I was in a meeting with my colleague Chris and Sam, the director of corporate real estate for our bank. Chris had created a product in five weeks that collected, analyzed, and displayed corporate real estate data. (This is an industry in which data is public but incredibly hard to find and manage.) Chris had hit a user acceptance rate of 90 percent with some of the biggest corporate real estate companies in New York. He was demoing the product for Sam when Sam leapt out if his chair, sending it hurtling backward, and screamed into Chris's face with his nose literally touching Chris's nose, "You're going to embarrass me with this shit!"

I sat wide-eyed and paralyzed watching this—not knowing whether or how to intervene. But Chris knew exactly what to do. "I quit," he said. And he left the room.

"You can leave, too," Sam said to me. "Fuck," he muttered to himself as I shuffled out.

Two weeks later, Chris founded a corporate real estate data analytics startup which today is worth $270 million. Sam didn't have a known cost of not innovating while Chris still worked for him. But once Chris quit and deployed the same validation techniques on the outside as he had on the inside, the cost of not innovating on Sam's part (and being an asshole) became very clear indeed.

3. You also just might be wrong. I have a fragile ego, and I unfortunately hate being told no. In my life as an intrapreneur, there have been many moments in which I have misdiagnosed legitimate objections as self-serving politics. The distance between strong user acceptance and a fully built and implemented product is incredibly hard to predict. The costs and difficulty of storing, transferring, and protecting data are hard to assess (even though they are declining). It may also be that in the process of achieving guerilla validation, you uncover a bigger organizational problem (like relationship hoarding) that needs to be addressed at a larger scale before your product can be built. Over time, I've learned to swallow these setbacks and appreciate their logic. At least, I try to.

Guerrilla validation, ultimately, is the process of taking a new product as far as you can as fast as possible. It requires a commitment to hunt for your target user wherever they may be and to try and see the world through their eyes. It also means being comfortable with early and inevitable failure. When it works, it illuminates a sharp contrast between bright possibility and suboptimal inertia. It holds the power structure of a huge company accountable in a way that is otherwise not possible. It's thrilling. But make sure to wear a helmet.

VI
—

INNOVATION ON TOUR SECRETLY

THE SPOTS

By the summer of 1977, the Sex Pistols faced a financial crisis.

As Her Royal Majesty Queen Elizabeth prepared to celebrate her jubilee, their lyric "God save the queen / The fascist regime" screamed from radios across the UK. As they spat on their audience, insulted the monarchy, and indiscreetly injected themselves with heroin, their fans transformed from curious observers to rabid zealots. The BBC was pressured into banning them, forming a virtual blockade on radio airplay. Local governments across the UK passed emergency zoning ordinances which effectively banned them from entering huge swaths of the UK and shut down their concerts.

The more popular they grew, the harder it became to earn money.

So in the summer of 1977, their manager Malcolm McLaren came up with a solution. He invented a new band: the SPOTS, short for the Sex Pistols on Tour Secretly. The pseudonym was discreet enough for them to play all nineteen of their scheduled shows, but not so discreet that they were unknown. The plan worked. Under this assumed identity, the Sex Pistols were said to have the highest grossing act in the UK.

NECESSARY MERCENARIES

Throughout my career, I have had to form different variations of the SPOTS: the PwCOTS, the BOTS (Bloomberg), the VOTS (Viacom). These teams do all of the work that is mission critical for the success of the product but would never get past the brand cops, the compliance cops, the software architecture cops, and all the relationship managers who block access to their prized clients.

Here's the thing: you have to do something like this to circumvent the corporate gatekeepers and demonstrate that a critical problem can be solved with an innovative product in eight weeks. There are certain important outcomes that entail taking risks that cannot be assumed by someone inside of the organization. They may be too controversial, too slow, or too politically fraught to be achieved internally.

For this reason, an effective intrapreneur must enlist external Mercenaries whose only job is to move fast, unencumbered by corporate constraints. At some point, someone very powerful will say, "That's amazing! How did you build that?" That is one of the intrapreneur's magic moments—when you reveal an alternative path to a critical outcome that was previously off-limits.

LOYALTY × HONESTY = THE TRUE VALUE OF A GOOD CONSULTANT

This, ultimately, is the value of a good consultant in an eight-week product launch. They have a singular focus on product success and are not susceptible to the organizational distractions that derail so many intrapreneurs. A loyal consultant doesn't care about getting fired because they were never an employee to begin with. They don't care about stepping on the toes of an executive who "owns" a particular client relationship because it's not their executive. And over time, they learn that their value only increases when they speak truth to power—even when it's not what people want to hear. Their only purpose is to demonstrate that there is a better way to think, build, validate, and grow. They build products that break through the enterprise Wall of Can't and illuminate that "can't" is usually a bullshit excuse from someone who actually means "won't" or "I would prefer not to."

This is what I now do for a living. The stated reason that huge companies hire me is to rapidly transform ideas into products. But there are lots of consultants who can strategize, design, build, and validate very quickly. That's not the primary reason they hire me. The primary reason they hire me is because they need someone external who can identify why they're unable to do it themselves. They hire me to speak truth to leadership that won't be heard unless it comes from an external expert. A good Mercenary doesn't just build a good product quickly. They also demonstrate that intransigence is an expensive choice rather than a default state. And they take the first difficult steps toward essential change.

I'm like a personal trainer who doubles as a therapist—except instead of individuals who want to get in shape, my clients are companies with 200,000 employees.

A SECRET SALES FORCE

One of the barriers to intrapreneurship that we've revisited throughout the book is the problem of relationship hoarding. Executives in huge companies carefully guard access to their clients even if the client is underserved.

Their status as a gatekeeper often acts as an insurance policy for poor performance.

A good Mercenary can go on tour secretly, build relationships with the client organization, and see if there are opportunities to cross-sell or provide better service.

One of my favorite Mercenary experiences happened with Time Warner Cable. I was working with a major bank that hired me to create a new software solution for the cable and telecommunications industry. At least, that's what they said they wanted me to build. In reality, they wanted me to find a way to bypass their senior executive, Mohammed, who "owned" the relationship with Time Warner Cable. The bank believed they were losing out on opportunities to cross-sell services to Time Warner. But Mohammed guarded that relationship like a ferocious Rottweiler. He made no secret that he would destroy anyone who approached them without his permission—which he almost never granted.

But I wasn't an employee of the bank. My only job was to build new software in eight weeks and to introduce it to Time Warner. I didn't care about getting into trouble—in fact, it was my explicit mandate to bypass the gatekeeper and to see what would happen once he was provoked. I didn't give a shit if he hated me.

And so I went on tour secretly. I networked my way into the executive level of Time Warner and arranged a meeting with Chris, a director of operations. He loved our early prototypes and arranged for us to run a series of user tests with his team. After three weeks, we hit a 90 percent user acceptance threshold, and Chris wanted to arrange a meeting with his COO to see if we could go into a pilot project. At this stage, he had no idea who had sent me. He had no idea that his COO was the other side of the relationship that Mohammed hoarded so jealously. All he knew was that, in three weeks, I had built something that solved a problem that he couldn't solve with the solutions he was using at that time.

This was excellent validation for the product that we were developing. But more importantly, it illustrated that Mohammed was badly mismanaging a key client relationship and holding the company hostage with it.

When Mohammed found out about our software with Time Warner Cable he was furious...but only for a day. The following day, he realized that he could either deliver what Time Warner wanted or lose the relationship. So he softened up and finally loosened his grip on the relationship.

A BRAND'S ALTER EGO

If you worked in a startup or digital agency in Los Angeles,

St. Louis, or New York between October and November of 2015, you probably saw an ad on Facebook for a new app called FirstMillion. This app was created by alumni of McKinsey and PwC and provided financial coaching to agencies and startups that Fortune 500 execs pay millions for. You may have read some advice columns from the founders of FirstMillion in *Inc.* magazine about how to reach profitability, survive without venture capital, and get clients to pay you on time. About nine hundred people attended one of FirstMillion's launch parties, where startup and agency founders partied all night long.

Nearly three thousand of you signed up to download the app.

What you didn't know was that I was FirstMillion. And it didn't actually exist.

My team and I had spent two months stuck in branding hell with PwC's marketing cops. We had amazing validation that startup founders and digital agencies badly needed financial management help and had no one to turn to. We developed an app that they loved. But if we wanted to launch it under PwC's name, we would have had to wait in line for the brand police. And they were terrified that we might break their rules.

So my external team, hired by PwC, invented a fake

startup, called it FirstMillion, and launched it. We wanted to measure and demonstrate the Cost of Not Innovating for PwC. How much user acquisition was the organization leaving on the table by moving so slowly and resisting change? We knew that we would never persuade them to get out of their own way until we showed there was a validated market that was waiting for them to change. And once we did, they had a lot more clarity about what to do.

Huge companies are extremely cautious with their brand. It takes decades to build trust in a brand, and if it's mismanaged, it can come crashing down instantly and sometimes permanently. Many corporate branding departments are so scared of a brand crisis that they prevent any innovative go-to-market campaigns from ever getting launched. Their caution is understandable. But it also means that they see risks that aren't actually there. Many great new products never reach the people who need and want them because they have to spend seven months with the brand team micromanaging the colors, font-size, imagery, and copy. It's hard to launch a minimum viable product without a minimum viable marketing strategy. This problem becomes more pronounced when you're trying to launch a social media marketing campaign in Google or Facebook where many companies haven't developed brand guidelines yet.

FirstMillion showed PwC what was possible if they were willing to change.

"WE'RE ACTUALLY NOT THAT DIFFERENT."

My partner agency, Philosophie, had a product studio on Twenty-Sixth Street in New York. It was chaotic, disheveled, and beautiful. Peter brought his huge, gentle pit bull to work every day. The walls were covered in Post-it Notes. Every whiteboard was filled with the remnants of the last brainstorming session. The ratio of beer to other stuff in the fridge was not normal. The air smelled of Sharpies. And Bad Brains, the Ramones, or the Yeah Yeah Yeahs were usually playing in the background.

It was very hard for our corporate clients to see what was possible if we were in their office. I was better at communicating our vision in that environment than most of us because I had spent so much time in big finance. But it didn't feel real to them until they saw us in action.

So one of the jobs of our client's Godfather was to invite other executives to come down from Midtown Manhattan to our studio to observe user tests and hang out for drinks afterwards. They would step off the elevator in their custom-tailored suits and Hermès ties, and step into our software beehive.

At first, they would be visibly uncomfortable. They would unbutton their top buttons and loosen their ties as we awkwardly shook hands. We would turn the music down to accommodate them. Then they would observe a user test that went well and share a few drinks with us. They began to see that we were motivated by the same goals and had a lot in common. They would start to see that there was a different way of working. In many of their minds, people like us were not people who they could relate to or work with. And yet here we were.

Good Mercenaries can help erase the perceived cultural divide that prevents intrepreneurs and corporate executives from finding common ground.

WHAT SHOULD (AND SHOULD NOT) BE OUTSOURCED?

The most important factor in determining what should be outsourced or kept in-house is speed. By the end of eight weeks, there should be an astounding, pronounced gap between the speed of the intrapreneur's product and the corporate status quo. Other causes of corporate stagnation, like politics, unstable technology, strategic misalignment, or process intransigence, all manifest themselves in the one supersymptom of slowness.

More specifically, by the third week of the project, you should reach a 90 percent user acceptance rate and triple the number of stakeholder supporters and marketing conversions. If you have an internal Entrepreneur Underground who can move at that speed, then use them. But most companies do not. And most companies that think they do actually do not. Once you begin talking with agile development or design agencies, you will quickly see the gulf between what you can do internally and what is possible externally.

One of the first and most important conversations to have with the Godfather is to identify what product outcomes are essential for solving a high priority pain point, accelerating user validation, and winning stakeholder support. These usually fall under the following categories:

- User acquisition
- User validation
- Technical stability
- Stakeholder validation

For each of these categories, the Godfather and product owner should identify which outcomes would require a sharp deviation from corporate norms in order to move fast. There are a few norms that aren't (or shouldn't be) up for negotiation: doubling value every two weeks, solving a mission critical problem rather than a safe problem, and not getting diverted by corporate constraints or norms. In this meeting, if you can't name specific people whom you can enlist and trust to achieve the outcomes that are essential, then you either need to cut the scope of the project or enlist an external agency.

One additional note on this point. If there is someone whom you trust from a cultural standpoint, but you're not sure they have the required subject matter expertise, you should only enlist them if they can work alongside an external consultant who would partner with and mentor them. Some of the most incredible breakthroughs of my career came when someone with the heart of an entrepreneur learned how to also use their head and their hands.

CREATE A NEW NORMAL—NOT AN ABERRATION

A critical concept for the outsourcing process is debt. Technical debt refers to the technology that needs to be created to make a product work that later needs to be replaced to support the product at scale. A very good proof of concept can be built with so much bad technology that its value is negated. If your company has an established and robust technology infrastructure that your product will need to integrate with, then it is important to minimize the amount of throwaway code that is deployed. Only write the code that's necessary to make it work. And be very clear about the code you believe will need to be replaced later. (Quick nerd sidebar: this is becoming much easier today because so much of software integration centers around creating and integrating APIs rather than huge, complex back-end integrations. End of nerd sidebar.)

The concept of debt also extends to strategic and process debt. I've worked on many great products that catalyzed astounding breakthroughs and then were unable to be reincorporated back into the company because there was no one who could manage them. Capacity building has to be an explicit goal of the project. It's great to outsource to Mercenaries, especially if the reason they are essential is because of willful obstructionism inside of the company. But if the reason they are essential is because of ineffectual processes or strategy, then there has to be an explicit goal to train and mentor internal teams. Otherwise the entire endeavor will be an aberration rather than a New Normal.

HOW TO CHOOSE THE RIGHT EXTERNAL CONSULTANT

A good consultant has the right combination of aptitude, capacity, attitude, and budget.

Aptitude—The most important determinant of the skillset you hire externally is the definition of *done*. A completed engagement may be as low tech as a PowerPoint deck or as high tech as a fully coded application. It also may mean that you have an internal team who is fully trained in agile or design thinking. If you have the resources to design a prototype but not to code it, then you will need to hire some developers or a development agency to take it to the next level. In my experience, the less risk there is of a botched handoff as a project goes from strategy to prototype to product the better. Make sure to carefully decide on the right endpoint for the product so that it can be handed off once it is complete.

Capacity—Do you need a person, an agency or a consultancy? If you have a seasoned, established intrapreneurial team who only need an extra set of hands, then you can probably hire a freelancer and save your funds. There's a huge difference in quality between a freelancer trying to make some money between jobs and someone who is a genuine solopreneur who is a master at their craft. Solopreneurs are harder to find and also tend to be selective about their clients because their business model depends largely on referrals. (WorkingNotWorking and Recorp are two resources where you can find high quality solopreneurs. Upwork is a good resource to find freelancers from across the spectrum.) Good freelancers are really good. Bad freelancers are hard to track down, require lots of micromanagement, and view clients as transactions rather than relationships.

An agency will typically range from five to one hundred people and will specialize in digital design, advertising and brand, software development, or industrial design. My three favorites are Philosophie, which is a full stack agile design agency (full disclosure: I've partnered with them on multiple engagements); Spring Design Partners, which is a user experience design agency in New York; and PointSource, which is also full stack with more of a focus on back-end architecture.

Consultancies like McKinsey, Capgemini, or Deloitte are typically not quite right for this type of engagement. Their engagements are usually very large scale and last for many years rather than the quick-strike eight-week product launch that we've been talking about. But they have also changed quite a bit and have been building huge digital practices that may be able to engage after an eight-week launch when the results need to be scaled across the company.

One final note on capacity. Over time, many top designers, developers, and product strategists (like me) choose not to manage anyone or be managed by anyone and leave the consulting space to work as solo-preneurs. One trend which is emerging is the coalition model, where teams of seasoned solopreneurs who have worked together at the top agencies form a coalition to serve a single client and then disband after the engagement is complete. If you can tap such a group, you will typically find the top talent from the agency space but without having to spend as much money.

Attitude—There are two key litmus test questions that separate the right attitude from the wrong attitude.

- Can you describe an experience where you had to move forward with a lot of ambiguity and changing requirements?
- Who is your favorite colleague you've ever worked with? Who's your least favorite?

If their answers reveal someone who thrives in ambiguity, does not require micromanagement, and seems like a card-carrying member of the entrepreneurial underground, then you've found a good match.

Mercenaries enable intrapreneurs to bypass the organizational constraints that derailed previous efforts to launch. When they are effective, they achieve mission critical business outcomes in record time. They also illuminate a new way of thinking and doing that will create a New Normal for the company.

VII

—

THE RIGHT EXIT AND ITS EVIL TWIN

The Senior Vice President who ran Stephanie Trunzo's division at IBM arrived for their lunch a little late with a grin that barely concealed that he had big news.

"Hi John, you seem joyful today," Stephanie said.

"I'm just excited about the great product release you've pulled off, Stephanie," John came back with a mischievous smile.

"You know I hate the drama. Tell me what you're smiling about."

"Okay, okay. Well, you're not supposed to know this for another seven days, so please keep this a secret. But the executive leadership team is over the moon with your last product launch, and you are in line to become director of the division. You're being called up to the big leagues!"

Stephanie clinked his extended glass and mimicked the role of someone receiving exciting news. "Wow! Thanks for all of your support."

John's enthusiasm for Stephanie's promotion was genuine and heartfelt. He was a loyal mentor and a good Godfather. Seeing her grow and witnessing the impact she had at IBM brought him authentic pride. Many times, he had gone to war to protect her and the products she built. And each time, she repaid his loyalty exponentially. He wore those battle scars like a Vietnam vet dons a commemorative baseball cap. "Don't fuck with Stephanie" might as well have been tattooed on his knuckles.

But John's announcement sent a poignant jolt through Stephanie's heart. A jolt that told her this wasn't what she wanted, like the way some people realize they need to end a relationship only at the very moment they are standing at the altar. The news gave her immediate clarity that she had to leave. With her latest project, she had a new sense of how impactful she could be. If she stayed, she would have to defer too many of her biggest dreams and settle for a paradigm of success that was theirs—but no longer hers. She felt like she was drifting from her best, most impactful self and wanted a span of control that was bigger than the guardrails of her current corporate world. Her next move, whatever it might be, had been something that she previously had pondered passively. But at that moment, it became a fiercely urgent priority.

Leaving proved to be one of the best decisions of her life. She went on to found PointSource, which was recently acquired by Globant for $28 million. (She and I have worked together on several products, which is how I know her exit story from IBM.)

DON'T SLOW DOWN

Stephanie's sudden awareness that she couldn't go back to her old life is a common outcome of an eight-week product launch. As an intrapreneur gains traction with users and accelerates change, they emerge with a new understanding of their own capability. And they feel a sudden urgency to not delay.

Once you complete an eight-week sprint, make sure that you negotiate the next move based on your definition of success—not theirs. This may mean leaving money and status on the table. It may mean that you take on a heightened level of risk and uncertainty. It's scary. And I've never known any intrapreneur who regretted that decision. Not one.

Warren Buffett said it best: "I think you are out of your mind if you keep taking jobs that you don't like because you think it will look good on your résumé. Isn't that a little like saving up for sex when you're old?"

For a company, the cost of not innovating is the financial pain they will experience if nothing changes. But for the intrapreneur, the cost of not innovating is the cost of deferring their impact on modernity.

By the end of an eight-week product launch, you will see a huge reservoir of pent-up demand for you and your product. Many assumptions about your customer, your company, and yourself will be rewired. You will quickly learn that the market places greater value on someone who can reach a 90 percent user acceptance rate in eight weeks than someone who will be promoted if they keep their head down and their nose clean. An innovator who can uncover an unmet user need and catalyze exponential growth with a new solution possesses a distinct competitive advantage in today's economy over someone who can sustain linear growth for an old business. And a Godfather who can empower previously invisible talent and reduce the cost of not innovating is more valuable than an executive who tries to freeze obsolete hierarchy while grabbing and protecting territory.

A hard truth that comes into glaring focus is the extent to

which your old life was divorced from building anything that anyone actually needed. Once you're running ten user tests a week, you quickly see that no one outside of your company cares about who got promoted to managing director or that a factional civil war is breaking out between an old and a new guard. They only care about not spending money on stupid shit. And they're merciless once they believe that their loyalty is being taken for granted. An eight-week product launch illuminates exactly how a market will abandon a company that can't get out of its own way.

Against this backdrop, a successful exit is not straightforward. There is inevitable tension between personal fulfillment, product acceleration, and organizational change that needs to be reconciled to determine the best option.

But above all of these factors, there is one doctrine that is more important than all of the others: don't slow down. You can't go back to your old life and pretend the eight-week launch never happened. Everyone I know who gets seduced by a raise or a promotion and walks away from high-speed impactfulness regrets it. Actually, it's bigger than regret. They experience a soul-crushing sense of self-imposed subjugation. Their career quickly feels like a dream deferred.

So please, don't slow down. The universe needs you.

The complexity of finding the right exit is compounded by the fact that there is no settled definition of what an intrapreneur exit actually is. When a startup is successful, its final destination rarely deviates from three endpoints: they get acquired, go public, or stay autonomous and grow organically. But an intrapreneur exit consists of many more options.

Another layer of complexity is that every good intrapreneur exit has an evil twin. There is always a second option that looks alike but is really co-option disguised as promotion.

To help provide clarity, I developed the IPO framework for an intrapreneur exit. This framework assesses the right level of alignment between the individual, the product, and the organization (hence IPO). If you achieve the right level of user and stakeholder validation, then three outcomes will emerge:

- **Individual**—The intrapreneur has a clear sense of fulfilling, accelerated impactfulness. They know that they are solving an entrenched problem and are supported by a Godfather and a team of other intrapreneurs.
- **Product**—The product is solving an important unmet need in a differentiated way. There is a clear inflection point that has begun to emerge showing that user

acquisition, validation, and sales will grow in multiples and exponents rather than percentage points.

- **Organization**—The organization has a new sense of urgency about innovation. A new way of thinking, building, and doing will become the New Normal, and a new generation of leaders will be empowered to catalyze this change.

But these outcomes are rarely all achieved at the same time. In the following table, I illustrate seven intrapreneur exits.

	INDIVIDUAL	PRODUCT	ORGANIZATION
NEW NORMAL	✓	✓	✓
SPINOFF	✓	✓	✓
BEAR HUG		✓	✓
QUARANTINE	✓		✓
OUTCAST	✓	✓	
HONORABLE DISCHARGE	✓		
RUN TO FREEDOM	✓		

THE NEW NORMAL AND ITS EVIL TWIN, THE BEAR HUG

THE NEW NORMAL

In this scenario, the Godfather and the intrapreneur have achieved total aligned validation between users and stakeholders. Together they have solved a mission critical problem for the market and the organization and have full organizational support to make it grow.

The organization is fully committed to incorporate the process that made it work into other products where there is a high cost of not innovating. This also means that historically untouchable leaders and fiefdoms are dismantled and replaced with new, more entrepreneurial talent. The intrapreneur is given enormous power and autonomy and has a commitment from executive leadership to provide all the political, strategic, and financial support that is necessary.

THE BEAR HUG

The Bear Hug is the New Normal's evil twin. On the surface, the Bear Hug looks a lot like a New Normal. The intrapreneur is congratulated and promoted and given more resources to keep expanding. But soon, all the punk sensibilities that catalyzed the product's initial success are suffocated and killed. The Godfather is marginalized, often through a promotion that separates them from the intrapreneur and the product. The new designers and developers the intrapreneur must now work with are a far cry from the Entrepreneur Underground (and are often offshore). Scrappy startup talent is often upgraded and replaced with high-priced consultants from McKinsey and BCG or a huge software consultancy like Accenture or Capgemini. Soon, the energy and speed of the entire team slows to a lumbering, risk-averse, politically fraught crawl.

The Bear Hug is essentially regression disguised as promotion.

One way to avoid the Bear Hug is to imagine your worst-case Bear Hug scenario before you start and challenge your company to prove that they will prevent it from materializing. Ask difficult, deliberately provocative questions from the outset and see how people react. Stephen Gates, the head of design for Citi (about whom I wrote in Chapter 4), asked in his interview why they wouldn't close every branch and make it a completely digital bank. And he didn't ask nicely. He asked it with deliberate snarkiness. Not because he thought they should—but because he wanted to see how they reacted. They responded by asking him to convince them why he thought it made sense. (As opposed to ending the interview.) He needed to simulate disagreement before he could agree to take the job. The other way to avoid the Bear Hug is to name your terms about hiring, firing, and product strategy and to ask that they be put in writing. If at any point someone says, "Trust me," or "as a friend" instead of putting it in writing—then they are lying to you.

THE SPINOFF, THE OUTCAST, AND THEIR EVIL TRIPLET, THE QUARANTINE

THE SPINOFF

In this scenario, the new product and the team that built it are set up as a new stand-alone company with funding and support from the parent company. The intrapreneur runs this new entity, and typically the Godfather will become the chairman or stay involved as the chief liaison from the parent company. The parent company will usually wholly own this new entity or will retain a majority stake. The parent company may also raise capital from other investors.

A spinoff is the best possible end-result for many intrapreneurs. In effect, the parent company says, "We love you and your product, and we want to participate in your growth without getting in your way." The organization explicitly recognizes that they can't run every product like this—but that shouldn't end the relationship. In effect, the company embraces the team and their product but defers sweeping organizational change to another date and time.

THE OUTCAST

Some of the greatest startups of our time began as products that were cast out of huge companies. When a company says, "You, your product, and your asshole punk staff are all fired!" you have become an outcast. It essentially means that you and your product's user validation were not matched by stakeholder validation. The body rejected the organ. It often occurs when an internal team with a rival, incumbent product throws an apoplectic fit when they see what you've built and brought to market—and use this as the premise for getting you fired. It is also often a direct result of an intrapreneur and their Godfather saying no when given the offer of a Bear Hug. (Ironically, Bloomberg began life as a startup outcast after Mike Bloomberg and Tom Secunda were fired from Salomon Brothers. Lynda.com and Brooklyn Brewery also began life as outcasts.)

Every intrapreneur I know who was outcast suffered a bruised ego and then went on to do the greatest work of their life. It is a new beginning disguised as a bitter end. The Outcast often appears to be the Spinoff's evil triplet, but it is often the best possible outcome.

THE QUARANTINE

The quarantine is the Spinoff's real evil twin. In this scenario, the organization effectively says, "We love what you've done and want you to build a new innovation lab." This may seem like a flattering compliment, but it is usually designed to thwart innovation rather than accelerate it. The true intent of the quarantine is to separate the intrapreneur from the core business and the cost of not innovating. Many of these labs work with new cutting-edge technology like AI and the blockchain, and never use it to solve a single real-world problem. An intrapreneur in an innovation lab will soon feel the soul-crushing sense of wasting time and stagnating (albeit while also wearing a virtual reality headset).

HONORABLE DISCHARGE AND ITS EVIL TWIN, THE SCARLET LETTER

HONORABLE DISCHARGE

In this scenario, your Godfather takes you out for lunch, orders a bottle of something fancy, and says, "You're capable of amazing work, and we're holding you back. It's time for you to move on, and I'll orchestrate a severance package so that you can take your time and figure out your next steps. The organizational goals we set are not realistic, and I don't want you to waste your time or your talent trying to change a company that won't change. We/I want to support you in whatever's next and want to stay friends."

The Honorable Discharge also often works in the other direction. The intrapreneur takes the Godfather out for lunch and explains that it's time to move on. Most people who are honorably discharged after an intrapreneur sprint realize that they are entrepreneurs and not intrapreneurs. It often is the final invalidation that confirms that they are not cut out for the corporate life. In this scenario, the Godfather and the entrepreneur stay very close even after they no longer work together, often for life.

THE SCARLET LETTER

In this scenario, there is no fancy bottle of wine or gracious sendoff. You're summoned by HR on a Friday afternoon and told to pack your shit so that security can escort you out of the building. Or you quit—effective immediately. At the moment, this feels like you are being tattooed with a Scarlet Letter and will be permanently stigmatized. The truth is that I have never met a single intrapreneur who didn't view this moment as a blessing, albeit with risk and uncertainty that was terrifying.

The day before I quit my job at Bloomberg, I was at a friend's party when someone asked me what I did for a living. I sheepishly replied, "I run Innovation at Bloomberg, and I'm going to quit my job tomorrow."

"That's so badass!" she replied. "Do you have another job lined up?"

"No." I said, still sheepish.

"That's even more badass!"

I very quickly learned that the Scarlet Letter actually serves as valuable currency as long as you own it. When you're totally candid about why it didn't work out and the real work you want to do, people respect the authenticity and tenacity. When people hear what you've done, they respect the courage and open up their network to help you out.

You will emerge from an eight-week product launch with

new political capital inside of your company and new value outside of it. In order to capitalize on that value, you must commit to not slowing down. Whether the right next move is to stay or to leave is largely determined by how fast you can move. The right exit for an intrapreneur is the one that promises the most continued acceleration.

VIII

—

COURAGE AND RISK

THE MIRAGE OF RISK

By December 2012, I recognized that I needed to leave my job at Bloomberg. I felt stagnant, despondent, and unfulfilled. Yet I stayed there for another eighteen months because I was terrified that a wall of Horrible Outcomes would crash upon me if I left.

I was afraid to leave without a new job waiting for me. I was afraid to give up my benefits. I was worried that I would look bad for quitting. I was terrified that my savings were inadequate. And each negotiation to work with a startup fell apart when we started to talk about money and equity. I was worried that I would never make enough money again.

This career doomsday scenario was foremost on my mind

as I took the E train to Manhattan to hand in my resignation on a freezing January morning in 2014. I arranged a meeting with my department director and nervously recited my lines.

"Julie," I said when we met, "there are people who love it here and do great work here. And I'm proud to have worked with them—but I am not one of them. It's time for me to move on. So I am handing in my notice."

She did not leap out of her seat, scream at me, and threaten to sue me. She smiled, thanked me for all that I had done, and gave me a huge hug. She then called HR and asked them to extend my benefits for a month.

This was the first indication that the fears that had kept me chained to a job I hated were false. Soon, all of the other fears were discredited, too.

When I told people that I had quit my job without finding another new job, they responded with admiration rather than condemnation. The night after I quit, I was asked to introduce myself to a large crowd at a networking event. "I'm Greg Larkin, and today I quit my job as a director in Bloomberg's Innovation Team." The crowd erupted in applause.

When I finally landed my first consulting engagement with

Viacom, they offered me twice as much money as I had ever made in a month. My next client doubled Viacom's offer. Within a year, I was not financially destitute—I was making more money than ever before.

When I finally started directly consulting senior executives in these companies, I was bold and candid about what needed to change. And they didn't scream at me and throw me out of their offices. They were thrilled to hear the fresh, honest perspective of someone who had been through it before and was more committed to authenticity than ego-coddling.

I share this not to aggrandize my career. There are still moments of scary, intense pressure. But fixing it is entirely my responsibility. That ownership is empowering and motivating.

All of the fears that kept me from making a critical change turned out to be small and manageable. And as I work with intrapreneurs, I see how pervasive this inflated misperception of risk is. It prevents great innovators from doing their most courageous work.

BE COURAGEOUS

Courage, ultimately, is the greatest distinguishing factor of effective intrapreneurship.

Behind every bold new product launched from a big company—where a market is transformed or a new generation of leaders is given a voice—is someone who had the courage to step forward and say, "I recognize that this is going to be hard. That powerful, entrenched interests are going to try to stop me. And I'm doing it anyway. Even if it gets me fired."

This is the single most unheralded act of bravery in the entrepreneurial world. When a startup demonstrates that level of vision and audacity, we know their founders. They have names like Steve Jobs and Elon Musk.

When an intrapreneur makes that stand, we see the ribbon-cutting ceremony or the jump in stock valuation, but rarely do we know the actual intrapreneur. My hope is that this book changes that. I hope that every new product built in every large company has an explicit goal to change the organization that incubated it rather than an unstated prayer that intransigence doesn't win.

Because every person I've ever known who made that stand looks back on it as the most important and valuable turning point of their life. Even if they got fired afterwards.

Be courageous. Even though it might get you fired.

ACKNOWLEDGEMENTS

There are many people whom I'd like to thank for making this book possible.

A messy collection of personal essays coalesced into a book when my friend Jarred Kessler introduced me to Tucker Max, who introduced me to his company that turns ideas into books. So, thank you, Jarred and Tucker. I also want to thank Jerry, Hal, Nikki, Kathleen, and everyone at Book In A Box who made this possible.

Stephanie Trunzo and Dan Sellars got religion when I shared my early chapters with them and graciously spread the gospel to some influential and talented friends. Thanks to Werner Kruck, Stephen Gates, and Arin LoPrete for sharing your experience and insights.

If it wasn't for my experience at Innovest, RiskMetrics,

MSCI, Bloomberg, PwC, Fareportal, Spring Design Partners, Nestle, or Google, I wouldn't have had anything to write. I especially want to thank Hewson, Laura, Matthew Kiernan, Emerson, Skot, Aliya, Morrissey, Tim, and Jake. I continue to feel inspired and proud of everything we built together and how it transformed people's lives.

Finally, I'd like to thank my family: Anca, Stefan, Tannia, Amy, Jake, Pauline, and my kids, Max and Rose. I hope that you can now explain what I do to your friends.

ABOUT THE AUTHOR

**GREG LARKIN** began his product-building life twelve years ago after nearly getting fired from an investment research start-up for predicting that the booming housing market would collapse. (He wasn't, and it did). Since then, Greg has built more than thirty digital products, generating millions in revenue for companies like Google, PWC, Nestle, and Bloomberg, as well as start-ups. In 2015, Greg launched his own consultancy, Bowery315, as part of his mission to help more good products enter the world. He lives in Brooklyn with his wife and their two kids.

Printed in Great Britain
by Amazon

76536332R00083